W9-BQT-647

letterhead &
logo
DESIGN 6

ROCKPORT

All rights reserved. No part of this book may be reproduced in any form without the written permission of the copyright owners. All images in this book have been reproduced with the knowledge and prior consent of the artists concerned and no responsibility is accepted by producer, publisher, or printer for any infringement of copyright or otherwise, arising from the contents of this publication. Every effort has been made to ensure that credits accurately comply with information supplied.

First published in the United States of America by
Rockport Publishers, Inc.
33 Commercial Street
Gloucester, Massachusetts 01930-5089
Telephone: (978) 282-9590
Facsimile: (978) 283-2742
www.rockpub.com

ISBN 1-56496-790-5

10 9 8 7 6 5 4 3 2 1

Design: Stoltze Design
Front cover images:
(top left) Designer: That's Cadiz! Originals, client: Bicycle Club of Seattle
(bottom left) Designer: Acro Media, Inc., client: Acro Media, Inc.
(right) Designer: Synergy Design, client: Mirador Pictures
Back cover images:
(top left) Designer: Henderson Tyner Art Co., client: Pam Fish
(top right) Designer: Korn Design, client: Hooch & Holly's Restaurant
(bottom) Designer: Kirimia Design, client: Kirimia Design Office

Printed in China.

letterhead &
logo

DESIGN 6

ROCKPORT PUBLISHERS

GLOUCESTER MASSACHUSETTS

DESIGN

intro
duction

An effective logo speaks directly and instantly. A logo, unlike a multi-page brochure or even a poster, must deliver the goods with minimal means. Well designed logos deliver the message and the essence of the business they represent. A letterhead system allows the designer a wider breadth of possibilities: clever printing techniques and the use of paper distinguish the most unique and dynamic systems.

In making this book, we opened hundreds of envelopes and sifted through countless submissions: in them we discovered the diverse range of logos, letterheads, envelopes, business cards, disk stickers, and packaging labels that fill this book with thoughtful and sophisticated work.

We probably could have filled the whole book with Art Chantry's handcrafted and streetwise logos. Avoiding digital means entirely, Chantry proves once again that good design is about good ideas, not the latest computer program.

Carlos Segura integrates [T-26]'s artistic and contemporary typefaces with traditional letterpress techniques to create well-crafted and dynamic letterhead pieces.

Hornall Anderson Design Works delivered an array of work for creative and professional services that incorporated a classic and refined use of typography and imagery.

We received submissions from all over the world—and found that sensitive typography, more than anything else, distinguishes a good logo or letterhead from a bad one. In the original printed material, the various weights and rich textures of the papers satisfied the sense of touch, as well as design challenges. Through embossing, die cutting, and letterpressing, the featured designers celebrated the letterhead as an object passed from one person to another.

We hope you find inspiration in this collection of fresh new work from many of today's best creatives.

– Chris Reese & Clifford Stoltze
Stoltze Design

Stoltze Design was established in Boston in 1984 by Clifford Stoltze. Over the past fifteen years, the multi-dimensional studio has evolved into a ten-person team of creative and business personnel. Preferring not to specialize, the studio has worked with a diverse group of clients, ranging from the software to the entertainment industry, including Fidelity Investments, Lotus, Nokia, Houghton Mifflin, Capitol Records, and Lego toys. An avid music enthusiast, Clif Stoltze is also a partner in the Boston-based independent record label, Castle von Buhler, designing all of the packaging as well as co-producing some of the projects. This has led to assignments for record labels as diverse as Matador and Windham Hill. Stoltze Design's work includes identities, collateral, publications, packaging, and website design.

Recognized for their innovative design solutions and expressive typography, Stoltze has received numerous awards from national design organizations some of which include the American Institute of Graphic Arts (AIGA), the American Center for Design, the Society of Publication Designers (SPD), and the Type Directors Club.

Published work appears in **Graphic Design America, Graphis Annual Reports, Typograhics 2 Cybertype** and most recently in **Communication Arts, Print** magazine, and in a June 1998 **How** magazine article, and **CD Design: Breaking the Sound Barrier.** Exhibited internationally in shows, Stoltze's work is also in the permanent collection of the Cooper Hewitt, National Design Museum.

logo and promotional folder
REYNOLDS DEWALT
printer

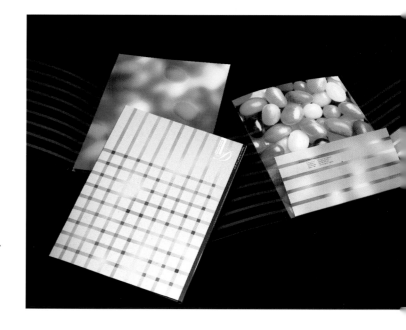

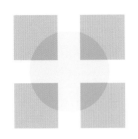

PLANET INTERACTIVE

identity system
PLANET INTERACTIVE
new media design group

identity system
OFFICE ENVIRONMENTS
office furniture dealer

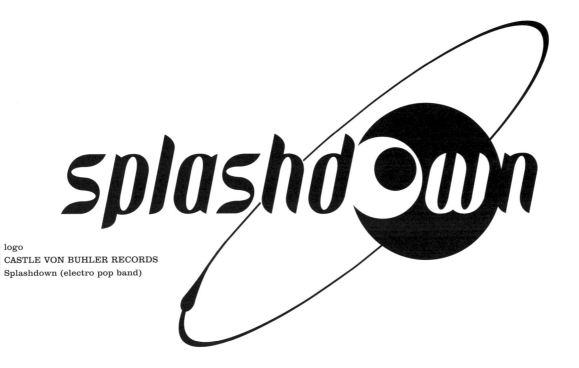

splashdown

logo
CASTLE VON BUHLER RECORDS
Splashdown (electro pop band)

identity system
FIRST SENSE
computer software company

FIRST SENSE
We See It Happening

wpa

Walker Thomas Associates

Catherine Thomas
Design Director

Walker Thomas Associates
Melbourne Pty Ltd
Design Consultants

Top Floor, Osment Building
Maples Lane, Prahran
Victoria 3181 Australia

Walker Pin

with compliments

KENNEDY

fax (515) 243

professional
services

860.659.8898

EMAIL
steepco@aol.com
steepco@juno.com

WWW
www.steep.com

ONE AND ONLY TEA MATCHBOX

PO BOX 89 ✳ SOUTH GLASTONBURY, CT ✳ 06073 USA

800 STEEPCO

PREMIUM LEAF TEAS & HIGH-IMPACT COCOAS™

design firm	Plum Notion Design Laboratory
designers	Damion Silver, Jeff Piazza
client	Steep Tea

design firm	Studio Hill
art director	Sandy Hill
designers	Sandy Hill, Emma Roberts-Wilson
client	Meyners + Co.
tools	Quark XPress, Macintosh
paper/printing	Strathmore Elements/ Black + Zhits Opaque White and Metallic Ink Temboss and Round Cornering

design firm	Hornall Anderson Design Works, Inc.
art director	Jack Anderson
designers	Jack Anderson, Debra McCloskey, Holly Finlayson
client	Personify
tool	Macromedia FreeHand

design firm	Studio Hill
art director	Sandy Hill
designer	Emma Roberts-Wilson
client	Tech 2 Me
tools	Adobe Illustrator, Macintosh

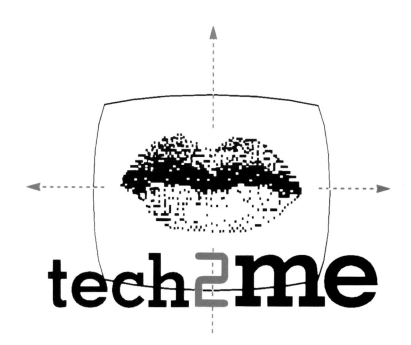

S T R A T E G I C   C H A N G E   M A N A G E M E N T

4329 E. McDONALD   PHOENIX, AZ 85018   PH 602 840-6509   FAX 602 840-7501

design firm | **After Hours Creative**
art director | **After Hours Creative**
designer | **After Hours Creative**
client | **Strategic Change Management**

S T R A T E G I C   C H A N G E   M A N A G E M E N T

S C O T T   J A C O B S O N

4329 E. McDONALD   PHOENIX, AZ 85018
PH 602 840-6509   FAX 602 840-7501
ScottJ01@aol.com

STRATEGIC CHANGE MANAGEMENT
4329 EAST McDONALD
PHOENIX, AZ 85018

design firm	**Bob's Haus**
designer	**Bob Dahlquist**
client	**Bruce Whitelam, Whitelam + Whitelam**
tools	**Macromedia FreeHand 5.5, Macintosh Quadra 800**
paper/printing	**Classic Crest/Lithography**

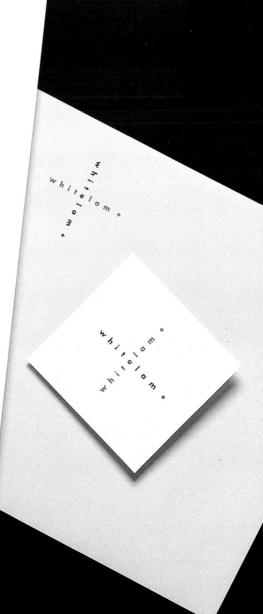

whitelam +

whitelam +

whitelam + whitelam

2102 19th street

sacramento, california

95818.1620

telephone: 916.444.1625

fax: 916.443.5783

e-mail: bw@whitelam.com

www.whitelam.com

whitelam +

bruce whitelam, a.i.a. and jacqueline whitelam, a.i.a. tout the firm's architectural expertise to clients.

design firm	Bob's Haus
designer	Bob Dahlquist
client	Bruce Benning
tools	Macromedia FreeHand 5.5, Adobe Photoshop 4, Macintosh G3
paper/printing	Classic Crest/Lithography

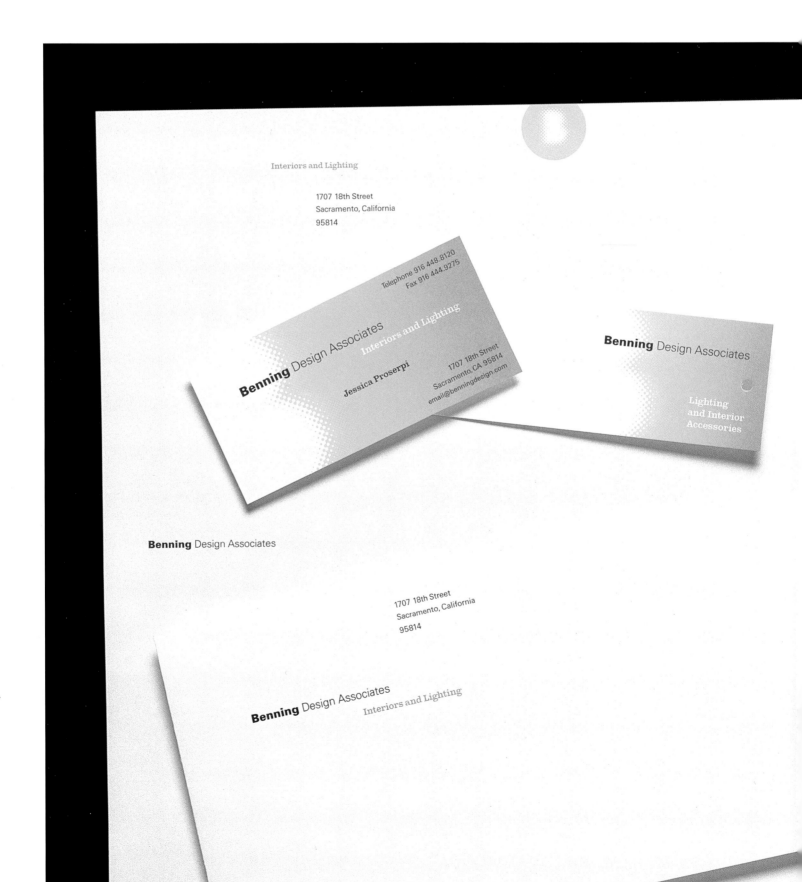

innoVisions™

design firm | Hornall Anderson Design Works, Inc.
art director | Jack Anderson
designers | Jack Anderson, Kathy Saito, Alan Copeland
client | Wells Fargo
tool | Macromedia FreeHand

design firm | Hornall Anderson Design Works, Inc.
art director | Jack Anderson
designers | Jack Anderson, Kathy Saito, Alan Copeland
client | Wells Fargo
tool | Macromedia FreeHand
paper/printing | 70 lb. Mohawk Superfine, Bright White Text

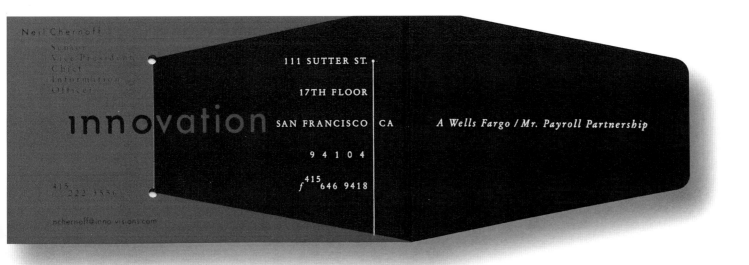

design firm	Visual Dialogue
art director	Fritz Klaetke
designer	Fritz Klaetke
client	Kent Dayton
tools	Quark XPress, Adobe Photoshop, Macintosh Power PC
paper/printing	Mohawk/Shear Color Printing

design firm	Vrontikis Design Office
art director	Petrula Vrontikis
designer	Logo and Stationary: Susan Carter
client	Levene, Neale, Bender and Rankin, L.L.P.
tools	Adobe Illustrator, Quark XPress
paper/printing	Neenah Classic Crest/Coast Lithographics

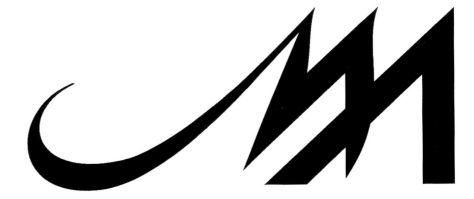

design firm	Studio Bubblan
art director	Kari Palmquist
designers	Jeanette Palmquist, Kari Palmquist
client	MA Arkitekter
tools	Macromedia FreeHand, Quark XPress
paper/printing	Storafine/Etcetera Offset

JASNA

JANE AUSTEN SOCIETY
OF NORTH AMERICA

ELSA A. SOLENDER
President

BARBARA HELLERING
Vice President

GISELE RANKIN
Secretary

GEORGE BRANTZ
Treasurer

NILI OLAV
Assitant Treasurer

BARBARA LARKIN
*Membership Secretary-
United States*

NANCY THURSTON
*Membership Secretary-
Canada*

RENEE CHARRON
Treasurer-Canada

LEE RIDGEWAY
Publications Secretary

design firm	Grafik Communications, Ltd.
designers	Kristin Moore, Richard Hamilton, Judy Kirpich
client	Jasna
tool	Quark XPress 3.3

JASNA

JANE AUSTEN SOCIETY
OF NORTH AMERICA

design firm	Nielinger Kommunikations design
art director	Nielinger Kommunikations design
designer	Christian Nielinger
paper/printing	Gohrsurühle, Zanders/Two color

JOHN MAHLUM · VINCENT NORDFORS · PATRICK GORDON · MICHAEL SMITH · MICHAEL YATES

design firm	Hornall Anderson Design Works, Inc.
art director	Jack Anderson
designers	Jack Anderson, Heidi Favour, Margaret Long
client	Mahlum
tool	Macromedia FreeHand
paper/printing	Mohawk Superfine Recycled White

design firm	Vanderbyl Design
art director	Michael Vanderbyl
designers	Michael Vanderbyl, Amanda Fisher
client	Rocket Science
tool	Adobe Illustrator 7
paper/printing	Starwhite Vicksburg/Expressions litho

design firm	Sayles Graphic Design
art director	John Sayles
designer	John Sayles
client	Big Daddy Photography
tool	Macintosh
paper/printing	Classic Crest Natural White/Offset

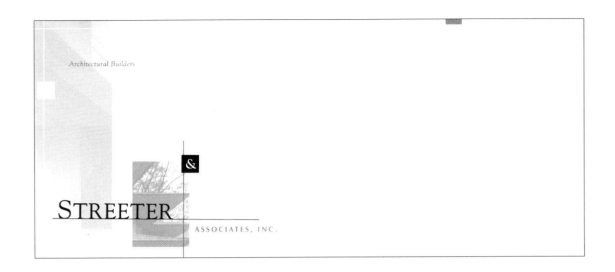

design firm | **Design Center**
art director | **John Reger**
designer | **Sherwin Schwartzrock**
client | **Streeter & Associates, Inc.**
tools | **Macromedia FreeHand, Macintosh**
paper/printing | **Classic Crest/Pro Craft**

Hengst Streff Bajko Architects

HSB

1250 Old River Road
Suite 201
Cleveland Ohio 44113-1242
e-mail: hsb@cyberdrive.net
216 566 0440 t
216 566 0229 f

design firm	Nesnadny + Schwartz
art directors	Timothy Lachina, Michelle Moehler, Gregory Oznowich
designers	Timothy Lachina, Michelle Moehler, Gregory Oznowich
client	Hengst Stregg Bajko Architects
tools	Quark XPress
paper/printing	80 lb. and 70 lb. Mohawk Superfine White Eggshell/Master Printing

design firm	Vanderbyl Design
art director	Michael Vanderbyl
designer	Michael Vanderbyl
client	Archetype
tool	Quark XPress
paper/printing	Starwhite Vicksburg/Archetype

design firm	**Walker Thomas Associates Melbourne**
art director	**Peter Walker**
designers	**Catherine Thomas, Neil Stockwell**
client	**Walker Thomas/Walker Pinfold Associates**
tools	**Quark XPress, Adobe Photoshop**
paper/printing	**Dalton Clipper Corporate/Four-color lithography**

Walker Pinfold Associates

wpa
LONDON

Walker Thomas Associates

Catherine Thomas
Design Director

Walker Thomas Associates
Melbourne Pty Ltd
Design Consultants

Top Floor, Osment Building
Maples Lane, Prahran
Victoria 3181 Australia
T 03 9521 4433
F 03 9521 4466
E wta@creativeaccess.com.au

Walker Pinfold Associates

with compliments

Associated Office

Walker Pinfold Associates
London Limited
Design Consultants

17 The Ivories
6 Northampton Street
London N1 2HY

Walker Thomas Associates
Melbourne Pty Ltd
Design Consultants

Top Floor, Osment Building
Maples Lane, Prahran
Victoria 3181

T 0171 354 5887
F 0171 354 0319
E wpalondon@aapi.co.uk

T 03 9521 4433
F 03 9521 4466
E wta@creativeaccess.com.au

Walker Pinfold Associates
London Limited
Design Consultants

17 The Ivories
6 Northampton Street
London N1 2HY

T 0171 354 5887
F 0171 354 0319
E wpalondon@aapi.co.uk

Reg. in England No. 238 6906

Associated Office

Walker Thomas Associates
Melbourne Pty Ltd
Design Consultants

Top Floor, Osment Building
Maples Lane, Prahran
Victoria 3181

T 03 9521 4433
F 03 9521 4466
E wta@creative.access.com.au

A.C.N. 066 086 888

400 n. 5th street, suite 1050, phoenix, az 85004
info@enx.com http://www.enx.com

steve chatham
consultant

400 n. 5th street, suite 1050, phoenix, az 85004
info@enx.com http://www.enx.com
voice: 602.257.7800   fax: 602.257.4457

400 n. 5th street, suite 1050
phoenix, az 85004

fax: 602.257.4457
voice: 602.257.7800

design firm	**After Hours Creative**
art director	**After Hours Creative**
designer	**After Hours Creative**
client	**enx**

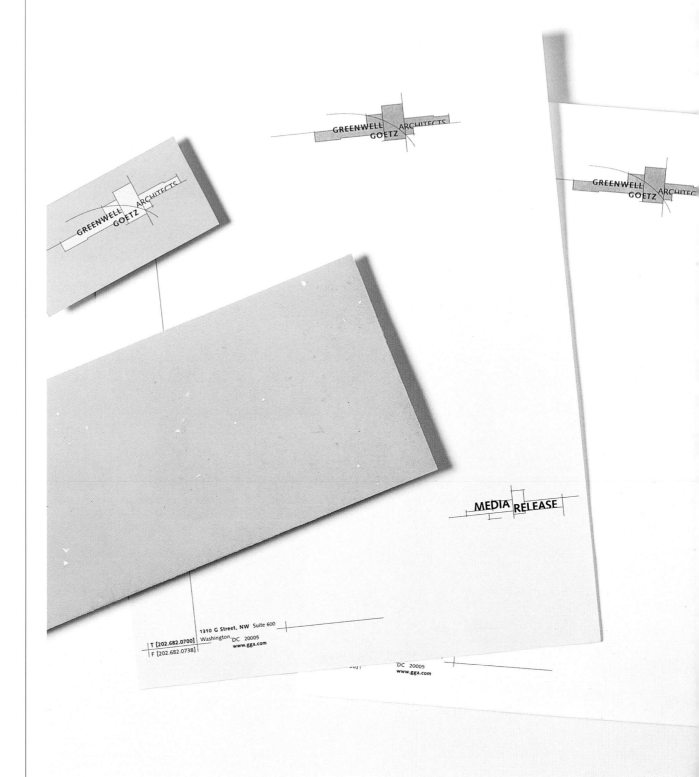

MEDIA RELEASE

1310 G Street, NW Suite 600
Washington, DC 20005
T [202.682.0700]
F [202.682.0738]
www.gga.com

DC 20005
www.gga.com

design firm	Grafik Communications, Ltd.
designers	Jonathan Amen, Regina Esposito,
	Gregg Glaviano, Judy Kirpich
client	Greenwell Goetz Architects
tools	Macromedia FreeHand, Quark XPress
paper/printing	French Frostone Frostbite and Tundra,
	Gilbert Neutech

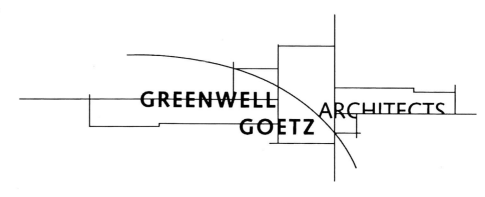

design firm	Modelhart Grafik-Design DA
art director	Herbert O. Modelhart
designer	Herbert O. Modelhart
client	Optik Mayr
tools	Quark XPress, Adobe Illustrator, Adobe Photoshop
paper/printing	Olin/Two-color, Business Card Cellophane

design firm	**Henderson Tyner Art Co.**
art director	**Troy Tyner**
designers	**Troy Tyner, Amanda Love**
client	**Place Photography**
tool	**Macromedia FreeHand**
paper/printing	**Strathmore Writing/Dicksons Printing Co.**

design firm	**Korn Design**
art director	**Denise Korn**
designer	**Javier Cortés**
client	**Pronto Product Development**
tools	**Adobe Illustrator 7.0, Power Macintosh**
paper/printing	**Alpha Press**

PRONTO PRODUCT DEVELOPMENT CORPORATION
22 Highland Terrace / Marblehead, MA 01945

PRONTO PRODUCT DEVELOPMENT

David Moschella

22 Highland Terrace
Marblehead, MA 01945
dmoschella@prontoproduct.com

T:781/631 1284
F:781/631 4360

ABA e com   *A subsidiary of the* AMERICAN BANKERS ASSOCIATION

► www.ABAecom.com   800·338·0626   1120 CONNECTICUT AVENUE, NW   WASHINGTON, DC 20036

design firm	**Focus Design & Marketing Solutions**
art director	**Aram Youssefian**
designer	**Aram Youssefian**
client	**Kogei, America**
tools	**Quark XPress 4.0, Adobe Illustrator**
	Adobe Photoshop 4.0

ABA e com

► 1120 CONNECTICUT AVENUE, NW
WASHINGTON, DC 20036

ABA e com

www.ABAecom.com

► 202·663·5387 PHONE   202·828·4532 FAX
1120 CONNECTICUT AVENUE, NW · WASHINGTON, DC 20036

design firm	Woodworth Associates
art director	Brad Woodworth
designer	Steve Westfal
client	Landmark Builders
tools	Adobe Pagemaker, Macromedia FreeHand
paper/printing	Strathmore Writing/Offset

design firm | **Karacters Design Group**
creative director | **Maria Kennedy**
designer | **Matthew Clark**
client | **Rick Etkin Photography**
tools | **Adobe Illustrator, Macintosh**
paper/printing | **Confetti/Broadway Printers**

design firm | Greteman Group
art directors | Sonia Greteman, James Strange
designer | James Strange
client | Austin Miller
tools | Macintosh, Macromedia FreeHand

design firm	Seltzer Design
art director	Rochelle Seltzer
designer	Louise Magni
client	Career Investment Strategies, Inc.
tools	Quark XPress 3.32, Macintosh 8600 Power PC
paper/printing	Classic Crest/Two color

CAREER INVESTMENT
STRATEGIES, INC.

CAREER INVESTMENT
STRATEGIES, INC.

ONE STATE STREET, SUITE 950
BOSTON, MA 02109 USA

ONE STATE STREET, SUITE 950
BOSTON, MA 02109 USA
TEL 617 720 2244 • FAX 617 720 2644

design firm | Insight Design Communications
art directors | Tracy Holdeman, Sherrie Holdeman
designers | Tracy Holdeman, Sherrie Holdeman
client | Rock Island Studios, Inc.
tools | Adobe Photoshop, Macromedia FreeHand,
Macintosh

VECTOR XXI,
Estudos de
Desenvolvimento
Económico e Social, Lda.

Av. Central, 45
Tel. 053. 616906/510
Fax 053. 611872
4710 Braga
Portugal

design firm | **Vestígio, Lda.**
art director | **Emanuel Barbosa**
designer | **Emanuel Barbosa**
client | **Vector XXI**
tools | **Macromedia FreeHand, Adobe Photoshop, Macintosh**

design firm	Nesnadny + Schwartz
designers	Mark Schwartz, Joyce Nesnadny
client	Fortran Printing, Inc.
tools	Quark XPress, Adobe Illustrator, Adobe Photoshop
paper/printing	70 lb. Champion Benefit Cream/Fortran Printing, Inc.

design firm	Warren Group
art director	Linda Warren
designer	Annette Hanzer Pfau
client	Candace Pearson
tools	Quark XPress, Adobe Illustrator
paper/printing	Strathmore Writing/Barbara's Place

(candace PEARSON) THE WRITERS' PROJECT | 2016 Valentine Street Los Angeles, CA 90026

213.665-0615 telephone

213.665-0990 facsimile

cp813@westworld.com

¹Halley's Comet.

²Indy 500. (THINGS THAT MOVE)

³San Andreas Fault.

⁴Candace Pearson.

CANDACE PEARSON IS PLEASED TO ANNOUNCE she has moved to new offices.

Same phone numbers. Same great copywriting.

ADS. ANNUALS. COLLATERAL. DIRECT MAIL. PACKAGING. PRODUCT NAMING. WEB WORK.

(candace PEARSON)

213.665-0615 telephone

THE WRITERS' PROJECT

A MODERN

2016 Valentine Street | cp813@westworld.com
Los Angeles, CA 90026

213.665-0990 facsimile

(candace PEARSON) | THE WRITERS' PROJECT
2016 Valentine Street
Los Angeles, CA 90026

A MODERN

(candace PEARSON) | THE WRITERS' PROJECT
2016 Valentine Street Los Angeles, CA 90026

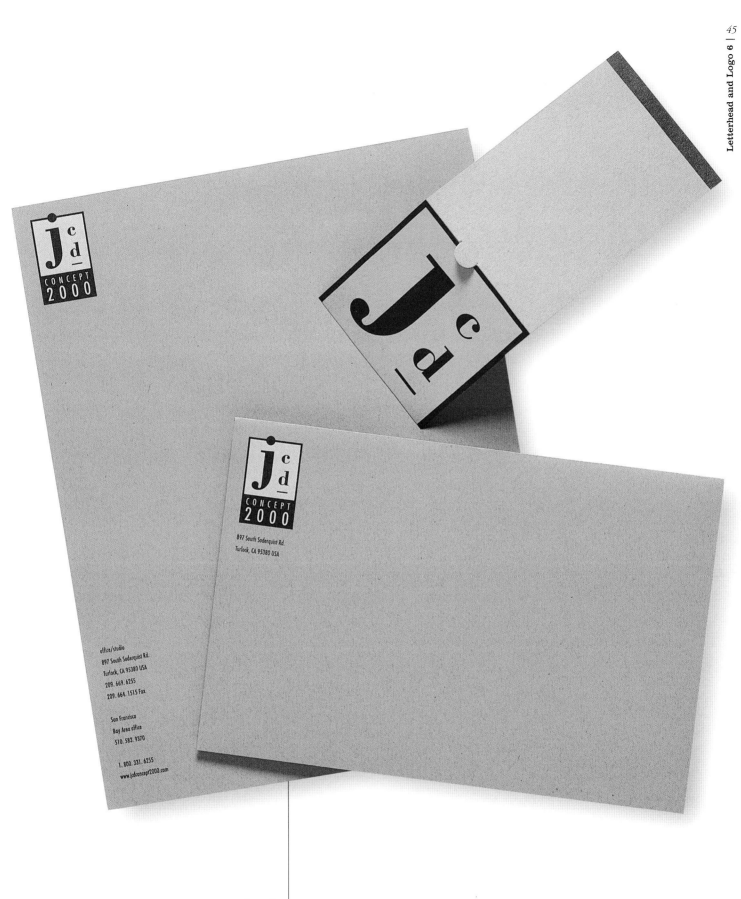

design firm	**Never Boring Design Associates**
art director	**David Boring**
designer	**Alexander Hillmer**
client	**JCD Concept**
tools	**Adobe Illustrator, Macintosh**
paper/printing	**Two color**

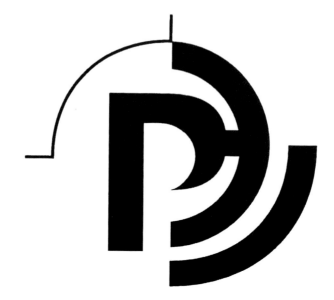

design firm | Fusion
art director | Barbara Chan
designer | Barbara Chan
client | Public Engineering Services, Inc.
tools | Adobe Illustrator 7.0, Macintosh G3

design firm | X Design Company
art director | Alex Valderrama
designer | Alex Valderrama
client | Rep File, Inc.

design firm	Earthlink Creative Services
art director	Aram Youssefian
designer	Barbara Chan
client	Earthlink Creative Services
tools	Adobe Illustrator 7.0, Quark XPress 4.0, Macintosh G3
paper/printing	Fox River Select/Costello Brothers Lithographers

Law Offices of
LANCE A. LICHTER

TEL
414 375-6868

FAX
414 375-6869

W62 N551 Washington Avenue Cedarburg, Wisconsin 53012

design firm	**Becker Design**
art director	**Neil Becker**
designer	**Neil Becker**
client	**Lance A. Lichter**
tool	**Quark XPress**

Law Offices of
LANCE A. LICHTER

TEL
414 375-6868

FAX
414 375-6869

W62 N551
Washington Avenue Cedarburg, Wisconsin
53012

Law Offices of
LANCE A. LICHTER

W62 N551 Washington Avenue Cedarburg, Wisconsin 53012

design firm | **Karacters Design Group**
designer | **Matthew Clark**
client | **Broadway Printers**
tools | **Adobe Illustrator, Adobe Photoshop,**
| **Quark XPress, Macintosh**
paper/printing | **Starwhite Vicksburg/Broadway Printers**

SPIN PRODUCTIONS TORONTO/ATLANTA WWW.SPINPRO.COM
620 KING ST WEST TORONTO ONTARIO CANADA M5V 1M6
TELEPHONE 416 504 8333 FACSIMILE 416 504 3876

SPIN PRODUCTIONS

KATHI PROSSER
ART DIRECTOR
kathi@spinpro.com

620 KING STREET WEST TORONTO ONTARIO CANADA M5V 1M6
SPIN PRODUCTIONS
WWW.SPINPRO.COM TELEPHONE 416 504 8333

SPIN PRODUCTIONS TORONTO/ATLANTA WWW.SPINPRO.COM
620 KING ST WEST TORONTO ONTARIO CANADA M5V 1M6
TELEPHONE 416 504 8333 FACSIMILE 416 504 3876

SPIN PRODUCTIONS

DALE SMITH
CREATIVE DIRECTOR
dale@spinpro.com

SPIN PRODUCTIONS

design firm	Spin Productions
art directors	Dale Smith, Kathi Prosser
designers	Dale Smith, Kathi Prosser
client	Spin Productions
tools	Adobe Illustrator, Adobe Photoshop
paper/printing	Plainfield Pinweave/CJ Graphics

design firm | Karacters Design Group
designer | Matthew Clark
client | Waldy Martens Photography
tools | Adobe Illustrator, Quark XPress, Adobe Photoshop, Macintosh
paper/printing | Domtar Naturals Kraft/Academy Press

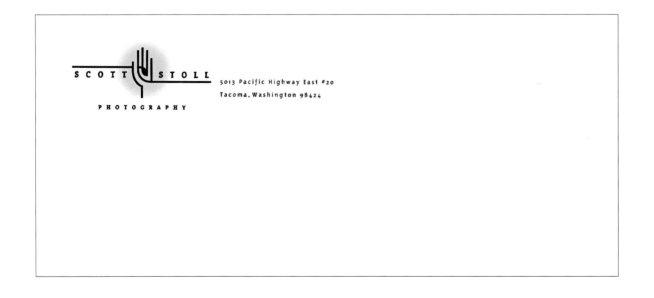

design firm | Belyea
art director | Patricia Belyea
designer | Christian Salas
client | Scott Stoll Photography
tools | Adobe Illustrator, Macintosh
paper/printing | Strathmore Writing Ultimate White

design firm | **Big Eye Creative**
art directors | **Perry Chua, Nancy Yeasting**
designers | **Perry Chua, Nancy Yeasting**
client | **Clarke Printing**
tools | **Adobe Illustrator, Adobe Photoshop**
paper/printing | **Starwhite Vicksburg/Clarke Printing**

www.dwl.on.ca

< DWL >

Tel: 416 410 1729 Fax: 416 603 4731
202 Euclid Ave Toronto Ontario Canada M6J 2J9

design firm | **Russell, Inc.**
art director | **Laura Wills**
designer | **Laura Wills**
client | **DWL, Inc.**

design firm | Greteman Group
art directors | Sonia Greteman, James Strange
designer | James Strange
client | R. Messner
tools | Macromedia FreeHand, Macintosh

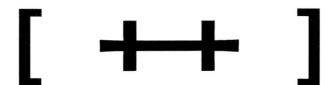

design firm | Barbara Chan Design
art director | Barbara Chan
designer | Barbara Chan
client | Husband & Associates
tools | Adobe Illustrator 7.0, Macintosh G3

design firm | **Russell, Inc.**
art director | **Laura Wills**
designer | **Laura Wills**
client | **Certicom, Inc.**

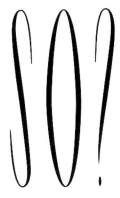

design firm	**After Hours Creative**
art director	**After Hours Creative**
designer	**After Hours Creative**
client	**Second Opinion**

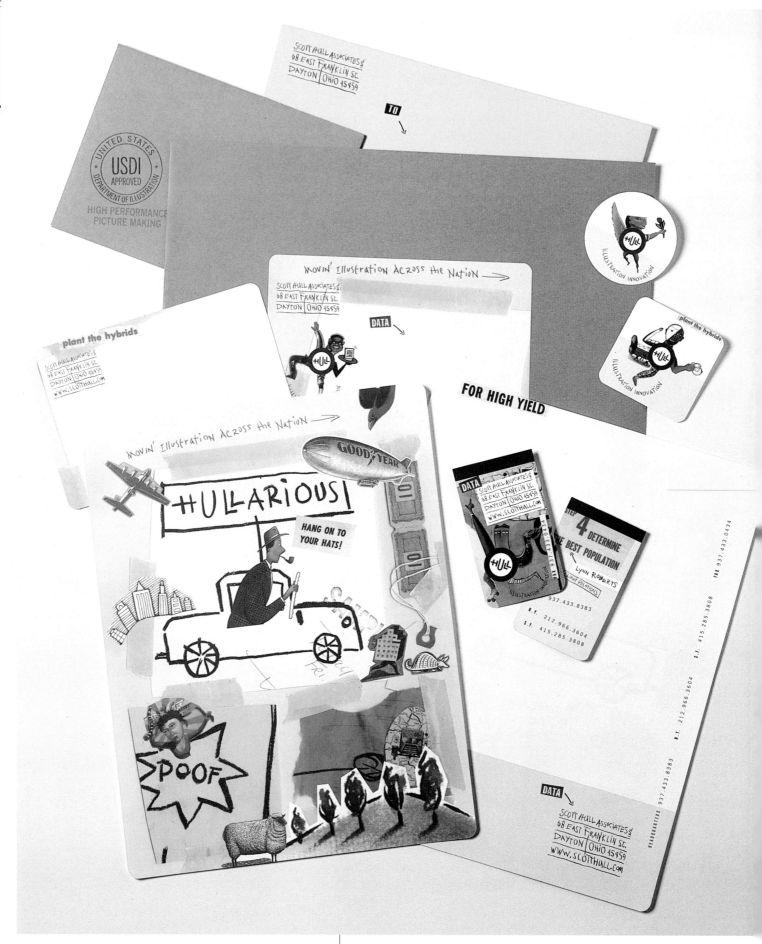

design firm | Siebert Design
art director | Lori Siebert
client | Scott Hull Associates
paper/printing | Arnold Printing

design firm | Russell, Inc.
art director | Bob Russell
designer | Laura Wills
client | Radnet, Inc.

design firm	Square One Design
art director	Lin Ver Menlen
designer	Lisa Vitalbo
client	Via
tools	Adobe Illustrator, Quark XPress, Power Tower 180
paper/printing	Strathmore Writing/D & D Printing Company

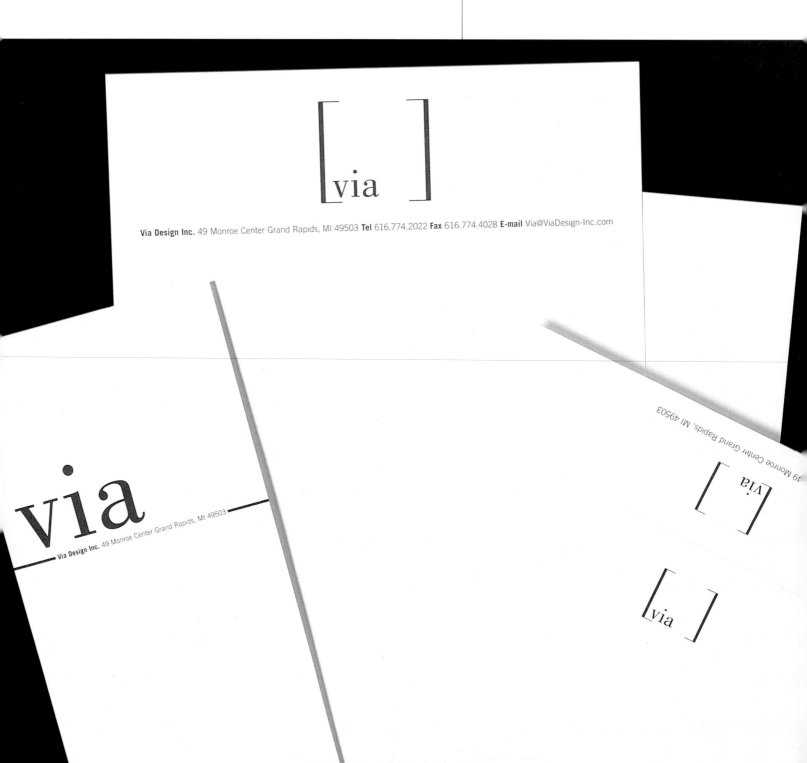

Via Design Inc. 49 Monroe Center Grand Rapids, MI 49503 **Tel** 616.774.2022 **Fax** 616.774.4028 **E-mail** Via@ViaDesign-Inc.com

Via Design Inc. 49 Monroe Center Grand Rapids, MI 49503

TMG classic mini radios

design firm | Jim Lange Design
art director | Genji Leclair
designer | Jim Lange
client | TMG
tool | Macintosh

design firm | Synergy Design
art director | Leon Alvarado
designer | Leon Alvarado
client | The Room
tools | Macromedia FreeHand, Macintosh
paper/printing | Vinyl/Silk screening

design firm | Choplogic
art directors | Walter McCord, Mary Cawein
designers | Walter McCord, Mary Cawein
client | Internet Tool & Die
tools | Adobe llustrator, Quark XPress
paper/printing | Fox River, Simpson Starwhite Vicksburg/
| Two-color lithography

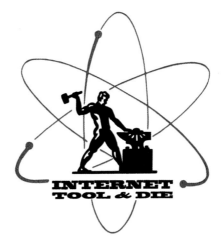

design firm | **X Design Company**
art director | **Alex Valderrama**
designer | **Alex Valderrama**
client | **Avrin Public Relations**

PROCESS SOLUTIONS

NEAL G. ANDERSON, PH.D.

129 UPPER CREEK ROAD, STOCKTON, NJ 08559
PHONE: (908) 996-2585, FAX: (908) 996-6505
E-MAIL: ANDERSON@ECLIPSE.NET

design firm | **Howard Levy Design**
art director | **Howard Levy**
designer | **Howard Levy**
client | **Process Solutions**

PROCESS SOLUTIONS

129 UPPER CREEK ROAD, STOCKTON, NJ 08559
PHONE: (908) 996-2585, FAX: (908) 996-6505
E-MAIL: ANDERSON@ECLIPSE.NET

design firm	Plum Notion Design Laboratory
art director	Damion Silver
designer	Damion Silver
client	Bikers Edge Bike Shop
tools	Adobe Illustrator, Adobe Photoshop

design firm	Han/Davis Group
art director	Ed Han
designer	Ed Han
client	Inform Research & Marketing
tool	Adobe Illustrator

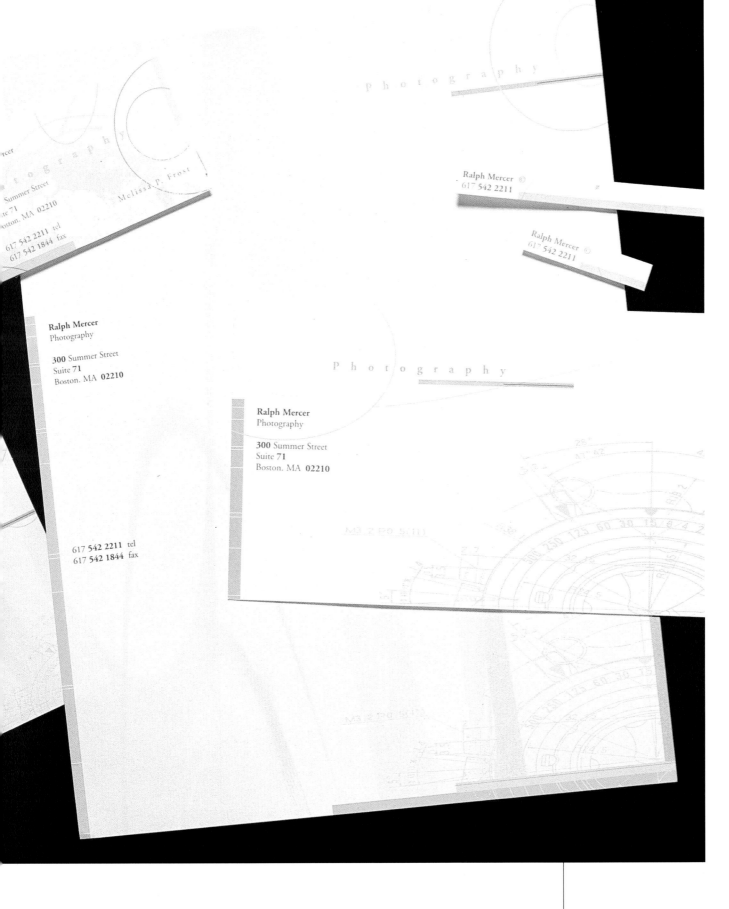

Ralph Mercer
Photography

300 Summer Street
Suite **71**
Boston. MA **02210**

617 **542 2211** tel
617 **542 1844** fax

Ralph Mercer
Photography

300 Summer Street
Suite **71**
Boston. MA **02210**

design firm	**Laughlin/Winkler, Inc.**
art directors	**Mark Laughlin, Ellen Winkler**
designer	**Ellen Winkler**
client	**Ralph Mercer Photography**
tools	**Quark XPress, Macintosh G3**
paper/printing	**Mohawk/Alpha Press**

design firm	Design Guys
art director	Steven Sikora
designer	Amy Kirkpatrick
client	Mike Rabe Music Engraving
tool	Adobe Illustrator
paper/printing	Gray Fine Art Paper, Beckett Concept Sand Text, Curtis Black Vellum Cover/Offset, Park Printing, Exceptional Engraving (Card)

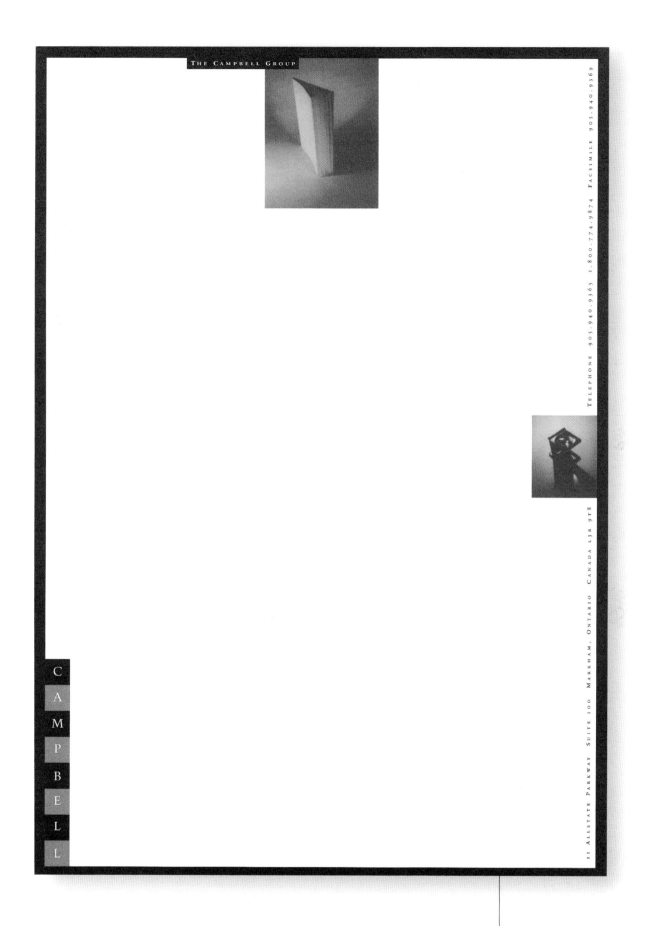

THE CAMPBELL GROUP

C
A
M
P
B
E
L
L

11 ALLSTATE PARKWAY SUITE 100 MARKHAM, ONTARIO CANADA L3R 9T8 TELEPHONE 905.940.9365 1.800.774.9874 FACSIMILE 905.940.9369

design firm	Vanderbyl Design
art director	Michael Vanderbyl
designer	Michael Vanderbyl
photographer	Michael Vanderbyl
client	The Campbell Group
tool	Quark XPress
paper/printing	Starwhite Vicksburg-The Campbell Group

design firm | **Hamagami/Carroll & Associates**
art director | **Justin Carroll**
designer | **Tony Mauro**
client | **Twentieth-Century Fox**

design firm | **Hamagami/Carroll & Associates**
art director | **Justin Carroll**
designer | **Tony Mauro**
client | **Twentieth-Century Fox**

design firm	Belyea
art director	Patricia Belyea
designer	Ron Lars Hansen
client	Belyea
tools	Adobe Illustrator, Macintosh
paper/printing	Strathmore/Artcraft

design firm | Design Center
art director | John Reger
designer | Sherwin Schwartzrock
client | Benchmark QA
tools | FreeHand, Macintosh

612 | 897.3505

BENCHMARK QA

America's Software Quality Assurance Specialists

7600 Parklawn Avenue, Suite 408, Minneapolis, MN 55435

E-Mail | BenchmarkQA.com

Fax | 612.897.3524

TREVOR SKILLEN *president*

METASOFT *Systems Inc.*

suite 203.1080 howe st.
vancouver bc v6z 2t1
tskillen@meta-soft.com

p 604 683.6711 *f* 604 683.6704

suite 203.1080 howe st.
vancouver bc v6z 2t1

p 604 683.6711 *f* 604 683.6704

designer	**Perry Chua**
client	**Metasoft Systems, Inc.**
tools	**Adobe Illustrator 6.0, Adobe Photoshop 4.0,**
	Macintosh
paper/printing	**Starwhite Vicksburg/Clarke Printing**

GENESIS INSTITUTE

#3 PLAZA FRONTENAC   FRONTENAC, MO 63131.3507   314.432.1772 FAX 432.2265

GENESIS

INSTITUTE

TIMOTHY JONES, MD

#3 PLAZA FRONTENAC

FRONTENAC, MO 63131.3507

314.432.1772 FAX 432.2265

design firm	**Bartels & Company**
art director	**David Bartels**
designer	**Ron Rodemacher**
client	**Genesis Institute**
tools	**Adobe Illustrator, Macintosh**
paper/printing	**Midwest Printing**

design firm	**Rupert Bassett**
art directors	**Rupert Bassett, Stuart Harvey Lee**
designer	**Rupert Bassett**
client	**Prime Studio**
tools	**Quark XPress, Macintosh Power PC**
paper/printing	**Mohawk Navajo/Offset lithography**

creative services

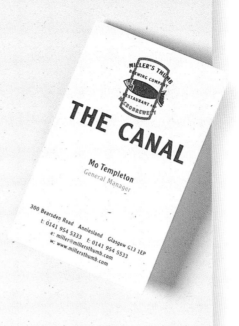

THE CANAL

Mo Templeton
General Manager

300 Bearsden Road   Anniesland   Glasgow G13 1EP
t: 0141 954 5333   f: 0141 954 5533
e: miller@millersthumb.com
w: www.millersthumb.com

10 Clairmont Gardens   Glasgow G3 7LW
t: 0141 331 7600   f: 0141 332 0336 · e: miller@millersthumb.com   w: www.millersthumb.com

design firm	**Teviot**
art directors	**Jane Hall, Kate Laing**
designer	**Jim Ramsay**
client	**Miller's Thumb Microbrewery**
tools	**Quark XPress, Adobe Illustrator 6.0**
paper/printing	**Metaphor Cream/Two-color spot lithography**

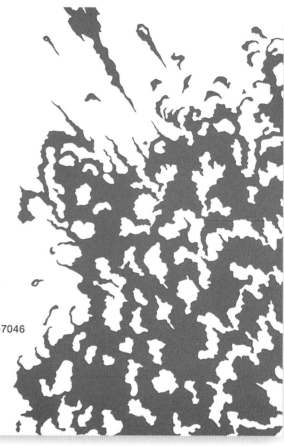

KIRIMA DESIGN Telephone 06-351-7045 Facsimile 06-351-7046

KIRIMA DESIGN Telephone 06-6351-7045 Facsimile 06-6351-7046

Yoriki-Cho Park-Bldg. 5F
1-5 Yoriki-Cho Kita-Ku Osaka-City
530-0036 Japan

キリマデザイン事務所
〒530-0036大阪市北区与力町1-5与力町パークビル5F

design firm	**Kirima Design Office**
art director	**Harumi Kirima**
designers	**Harumi Kirima, Fumitaka Yukawa**
client	**Kirima Design Office**

design firm	Shook Design Group
art director	Ginger Riley
designers	Steve Fenton, Dave Gibson
client	Walker Willhelm Productions
tools	Quark XPress, Adobe Photoshop, Macintosh G3
paper/printing	Classic Crest Solar White/Two-color offset

design firm	**Knezic Parone Advertising**
designers	**Joe Knezic/Mike Parone/Robinson Smith**
designer	**Robinson Smith**
client	**WireHead Business Technologies**
tool	**Adobe Illustrator**

design firm	Seltzer Design
art director	Rochelle Seltzer
designers	Rochelle Seltzer, Heather Roy
client	Seltzer Design
tools	Quark XPress 3.32, Adobe Illustrator 7.01, Macintosh 8600 Power PC
paper/printing	Astrolite/Two color (IPMS, ITOYO)

design firm | Hornall Anderson Design Works, Inc.
art director | Jack Anderson
designer | Mike Calkins
client | Hammerquist & Halverson
tool | Macromedia FreeHand
paper/printing | Mohawk, Navajo/Thermography on Business Card

Loja das Ideias

Rua do Campo Alegre, 1306
Salas 101, 102, 103 • 4150 Porto
Tel. 6069389/9402 • Fax 6007037
lojaideias@mail.telepac.pt
http://www.corimagem.pt/ideias/

design firm	João Machado Design, Lda
art director	João Machado
designer	João Machado
client	Loja das Ideias
tools	Macromedia FreeHand, Quark XPress
paper/printing	Fedrigonni, Marcata 140 gsm

Côr da Imagem

Rua do Viriato, 27 · 1°B   Rua do Campo Alegre, 1396   corimagem@mail.telepac.pt
1050 Lisboa   Sala 102 · 4150 Porto   http://www.corimagem.pt
Tel. (01) 315 1527 · Fax (01) 355 0942   Tel. (02) 609 3096 · Fax (02) 609 7037

Cor da Imagem

Rua do Viriato, 27 · 1°B · 1050 Lisboa
Rua do Campo Alegre, 1396 · Sala 102 · 4150 Porto

design firm	**João Machado Design, Lda**
art director	**João Machado**
designer	**João Machado**
client	**Côr da Imagem**
tools	**Macromedia FreeHand, Quark XPress**
paper/printing	**Fedrigonni, Marcata 140 gsm**

Ideias Virtuais

Rua do Viriato, 27   1ºB
1050 Lisboa
Tel./ Fax (01) 3556942
lojaideias@mail.telepac.pt
http://www.corimagem.pt/ideias/

design firm	**João Machado Design, Lda**
art director	**João Machado**
designer	**João Machado**
client	**Ideias Virtuais**
tools	**Macromedia FreeHand, Quark XPress**
paper/printing	**Fedrigonni, Marcata 140 gsm**

design firm | Henderson Tyner Art Co.
art directors | Troy Tyner, Hayes Henderson
designer | Troy Tyner
client | Henderson Tyner Art Co.
tool | Macromedia Freehand
paper/printing | Gilbert Oxford/Dicksons Printing Co.

design firm | Steven Curtis Design, Inc.
art director | Steve Curtis
designer | Steve Curtis
client | Steven Curtis Design, Inc.
tools | Quark XPress 4.0, Adobe Photoshop 5.0,
Macintosh
paper/printing | Strathmore Writing, Ultra White Wove/
Anderson Printing

design firm | Plum Notion Design Laboratory
art director | Damion Silver
designer | Damion Silver
client | Plum Notion Design Laboratory

5949 Sherry Lane   Suite 1800   Dallas, Texas 75225 | *Phone 214.378.7970   Fax 214.378.7967*

design firm | **The Point Group**
art director | **David Howard**
designers | **Crethann Hickman, Ridley Brown**
client | **The Point Group**
tool | **Quark XPress**
paper/printing | **Starwhite Vicksburg/Monarch Press**

design firm	Gouthier Design, Inc.
art director	Jonathan Gouthier
designer	Jonathan Gouthier
client	Gouthier Design, Inc.
tools	Quark XPress, Macintosh Quadra
paper/printing	Neenah Classic Crest Solar White/Joanne Miner

design firm	**Studio Hill**
art director	**Sandy Hill**
designers	**Sandy Hill, Alan Shimato**
client	**Studio Hill**
tools	**Quark XPress, Macintosh**
paper/printing	**70 lb. Mohawk Superfine Ultrawhite Eggshell Text**
	and 100 lb. Cover/Cottonwood Printing Co.

design firm | Designstudio CAW
designer | Carsten-Andres Werner
client | Self-promotion

DESIGNSTUDIO CAW

Carsten-Andres Werner | diplom grafikdesigner   kommunikationsgestaltung
Krugstraße 16 | 30453 Hannover | tel 0511.485.0295 | fax 0511.485.0299 | mail @designstudio-caw.de

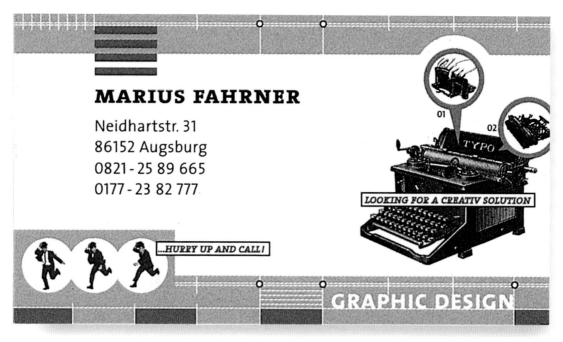

design firm	Marius Fahrner
art director	Marius Fahrner
designer	Marius Fahrner
client	Self-promotion
tool	Macromedia FreeHand
paper/printing	Ròmerturm Countryside/Reset Hamburg

design firm	Henderson Tyner Art Co.
art director	Troy Tyner
designer	Troy Tyner
client	Pam Fish
tool	Macromedia FreeHand
paper/printing	Strathmore Elements Grid/Topline Printing

mcg architecture

design firm	Selbert Perkins Design Collaborative
art director	Clifford Selbert
designers	Michelle Summers, Erin Miller
client	MCG Architects

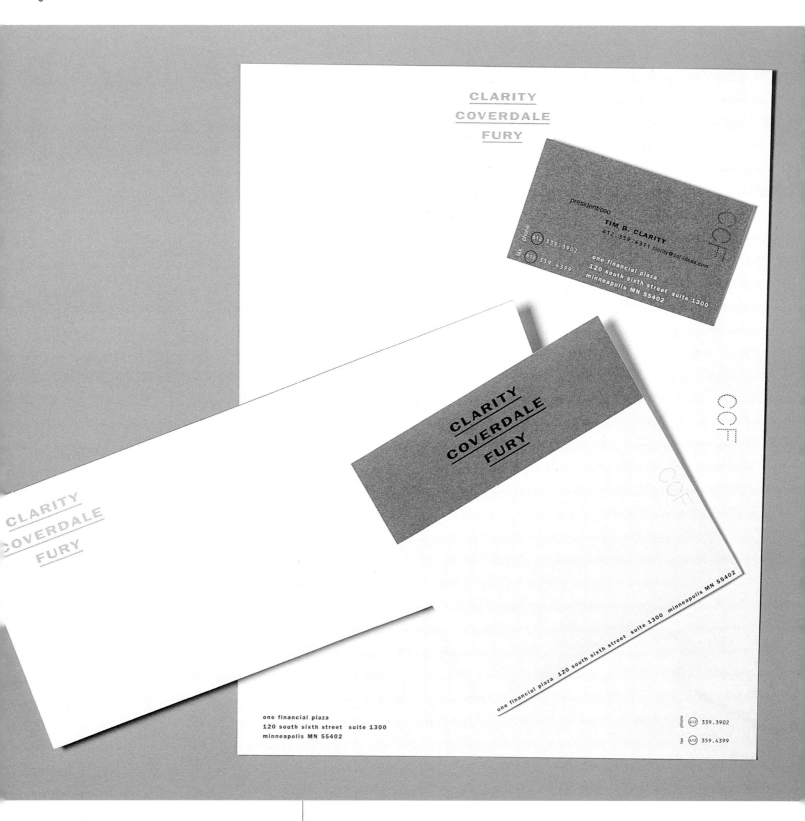

design firm | Parachute Design
designer | Cari Johnson
client | Clarity Coverdale Fury Advertising
tools | Quark XPress, Macintosh Power PC
paper/printing | Mohawk Superfine/Offset with Lazer Cutting on Detail

BLUE i DESIGN

design firm	Blue i Design
art director	Hellen Rayner
designer	Hellen Rayner
client	Blue i Design
tools	Quark XPress, Macromedia FreeHand, Macintosh
paper/printing	James River Classic Super Wove/ Cotswold Printing

BLUE i DESIGN

Imperial House
Lypiatt Road
Cheltenham
Gloucestershire
GL50 2QJ
Telephone: 01242 234500
Fax: 01242 253360
ISDN: 01242 221587
email: info@biuei.co.uk

Blue i Design Limited
Registered Office:
Roberts House
2 Manor Road Ruislip
Middlesex
Registered in England
No. 3437151

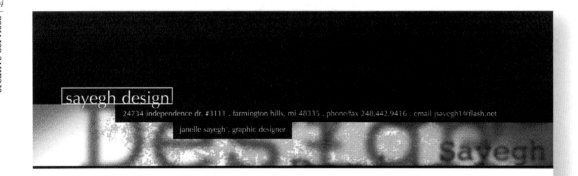

sayegh design
24734 independence dr. #3111 . farmington hills, mi 48335 . phone/fax 248.442.9416 . email jsayegh1@flash.net
janelle sayegh . graphic designer

design firm	**Sayegh Design**
art director	**Janelle Sayegh**
designer	**Janelle Sayegh**
client	**Sayegh Design**
tools	**Adobe Photoshop, Quark XPress, Macintosh**
paper/printing	**Neenah Classic Crest/Two color, Locke Printing Company**

janelle sayegh . graphic designer
24734 independence dr. #3111 . farmington hills, mi 48335 . phone/fax 248.442.9416 . email jsayegh1@flash.net

design firm	**what!design**
art directors	**Damon Meibers, Amy Strauch**
designers	**Damon Meibers, Amy Strauch**
client	**What!design**
tool	**Quark XPress**
paper/printing	**Ampad Engineer's Pad, Charrette Graph Paper,**
	Oxford Card Guides/Laser, Stamp Pad,
	Wood Cut Stamp Rubber Type, Embosser

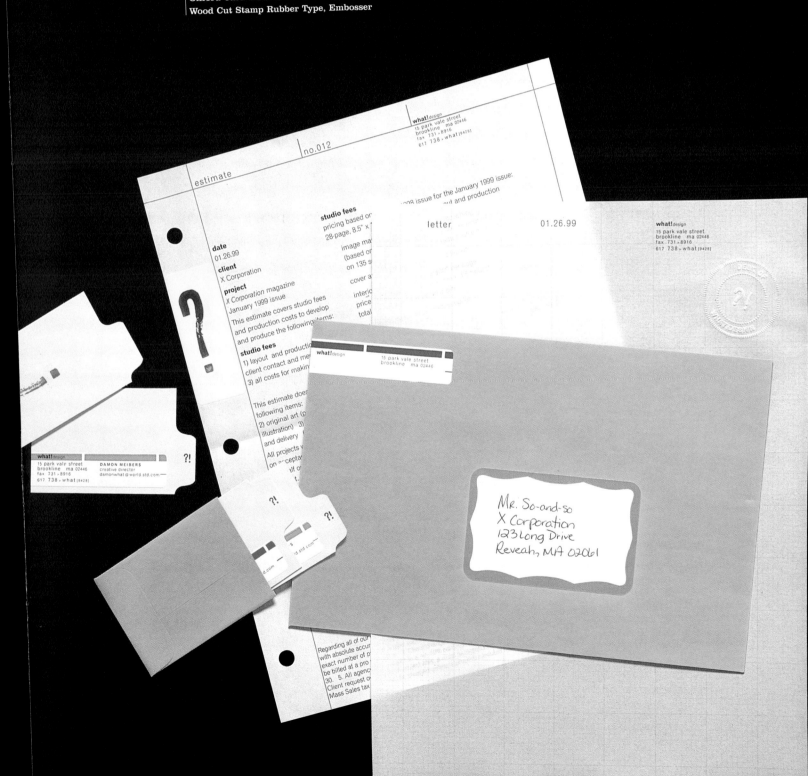

design firm	**Arrowstreet Graphic Design**
art directors	**Bob Lowe, Michele Phalen**
designer	**Trip Boswell**
client	**Arrowstreet Graphic Design**
tools	**Adobe Illustrator, Macintosh Power PC**
paper/printing	**Astrolite Smooth/United Lithograph**

design firm	Pham Phu Design
art director	Oanh Pham Phu
designer	Renald Strobel
client	Riesle Technological Consultants
paper/printing	Two color

lima design

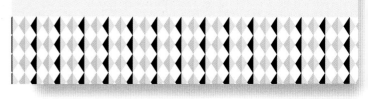

design firm | **Lima Design**
designers | **Lisa McKenna, Mary Kiene**
client | **Lima Design**
tools | **Quark XPress, Macromedia FreeHand**
paper/printing | **Monadnock Caress/Shawmut Printing**

PARDON OUR DUST
MCGAUGHY DESIGN
IS UNDERGOING RENOVATION
WE CAN STILL BE REACHED AT:
3706-A STEPPES COURT
FALLS CHURCH, VA 22041
703•578•1375 / FAX 578•9658
MCGDESIGN@AOL.COM

WE CAN STILL BE REACHED AT:
3706-A STEPPES COURT
FALLS CHURCH, VA 22041
703•578•1375 / FAX 578•9658
MCGDESIGN@AOL.COM

PARDON OUR DUST
MCGAUGHY DESIGN
IS UNDERGOING RENOVATION
WE CAN STILL BE REACHED AT:
3706-A STEPPES COURT
FALLS CHURCH, VA 22041
703•578•1375 / FAX 578•9658
MCGDESIGN@AOL.COM

design firm	**McGaughy Design**
art director	**Malcolm McGaughy**
designer	**Malcolm McGaughy**
client	**McGaughy Design**
tools	**Macromedia FreeHand, Macintosh Power PC**
paper/printing	**Various/Rubber stamp**

BIGBEATGROUP

10 clairmont gardens   glasgow G3 7LW

TEL 0141 331 7600
FAX 0141 332 0336
E-MAIL big_beat@compuserve.com

printed on recycled paper

big beat group limited   registered in scotland no. t37725

design firm	Scott Stern
art director	Jonathan Frewin
designer	Jonathan Frewin
client	Big Beat Group Holdings Ltd
tool	Adobe Photoshop
paper/printing	Four-color process, spot color, Spot UV varnish

design firm	Visual Dialogue
art director	Fritz Klaetke
designers	Fritz Klaetke, Chris Reese
client	Visual Dialogue
tools	Quark XPress, Adobe Photoshop, Macintosh Power PC
paper/printing	Certificate Stock, Starwhite Vicksburg/Innerer
	Klang Press, Alpha Press

G3 Marketing und Kommunikation
Dr. Bernd Gschwandtner
Dr. Adolf-Altmann-Str. 17
A-5020 Salzburg

T +43-662-832601-0
F +43-662-832601-13
E g3-marketing@salzburg.co.at

design firm	**Modelhart Grafik-Design DA**
art director	**Herbert O. Modelhart**
designer	**Herbert O. Modelhart**
client	**G3 Marketing und Kommunikation**
tools	**Quark XPress, Adobe Illustrator**
paper/printing	**118 lb. Strathmore Writing/Two color**

design firm	Lux Design
art director	Amy Gregg
designer	Laura Cary
client	Good Dog Design
tools	Adobe Illustrator, Macintosh 9600/300 Power PC
paper/printing	Starwhite Vicksburg/R.W. Nielsen Associates

design firm	Focus Design & Marketing Solutions
art director	Aram Youssefian
designer	Aram Youssefian
client	Focus
tools	Adobe Illustrator 7.0, Adobe Photoshop 4.0, Macintosh G3
paper/printing	Strathmore Writing System/Lithographix

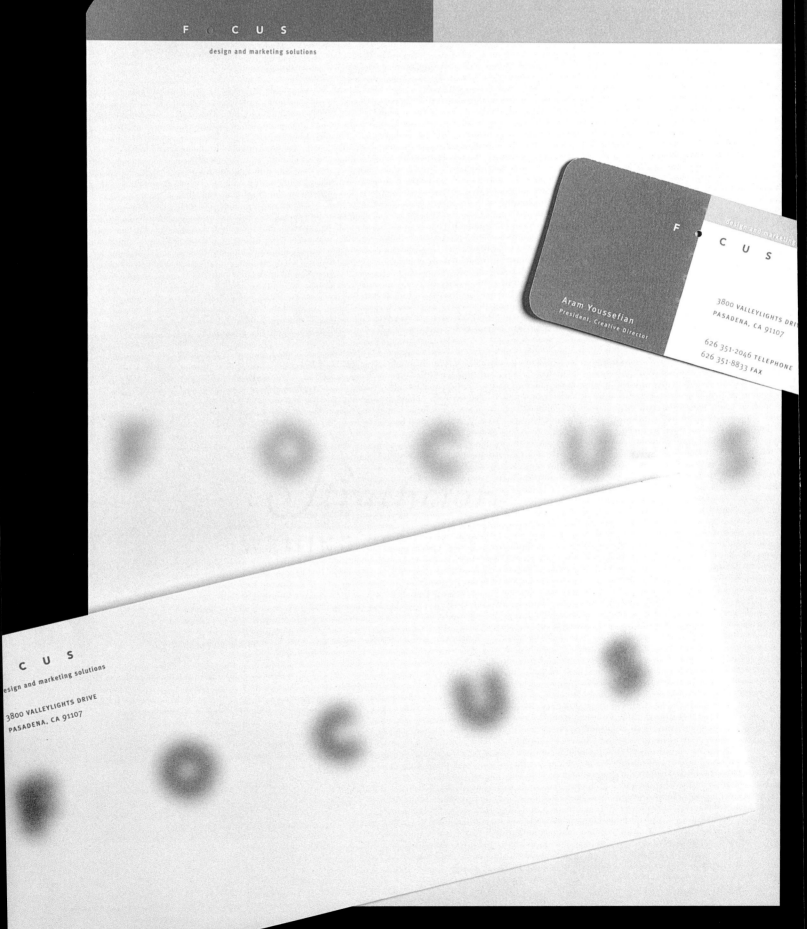

THE SOURCE OF THE FINEST
ARTISTS AND THEIR WORK

931 EAST MAIN STREET ▪ SUITE 3 ▪ MADISON ▪ WI ▪ 53703
PHONE 608.257.2590 ▪ FAX 608.257.2690 ▪ WWW.GUILD.COM

THE SOURCE OF THE FINEST
ARTISTS AND THEIR WORK

TONI SIKES
PRESIDENT

TSIKES@GUILD.COM
931 E. MAIN ST. ▪ STE. 3
MADISON ▪ WI ▪ 53703
PHONE ▪ 608.257.2590
FAX ▪ 608.257.2690

design firm	Planet Design Company
art director	Dana Lytle
designer	Ben Hirby
client	Guild.com
tools	Adobe Illustrator, Quark XPress
paper/printing	Neenah Classic Crest Natural White/ American Printing

design firm | Planet Design Company
art director | Kevin Wade
designer | Dan Ibarra
client | Brave World Productions
tools | Adobe Photoshop, Adobe Illustrator,
Quark XPress
paper/printing | Mohawk Vellum Warm White/
American Printing

1464-P1042A

design firm	**Planet Design Company**
art director	**Kevin Wade**
designer	**Martha Graettinger**
client	**CUNA**
tools	**Adobe Illustrator, Quark XPress**
paper/printing	**Classic Crest Ultra White/Lithography Productions**

SALISBURY STUDIOS

SALISBURY STUDIOS

design firm	Planet Design Company
art directors	Dana Lytle, Kevin Wade
designer	Raelene Mercer
client	Salisbury Studios
tools	Quark XPress, Adobe Photoshop

PH 608 256 5557   FX 608 256 5595

849 E WASHINGTON   MADISON, WI 5370

design firm	Modelhart Grafik-Design DA
art director	Herbert O. Modelhart
designer	Herbert O. Modelhart
client	Herbert O. Modelhart Grafik-Design
tool	Quark XPress
paper/printing	Strathmore Writing 118 gsm and 298 gsm/Two color

design firm	Lux Design
art director	Amy Gregg
designer	Amy Gregg
client	Lux Design
tools	Adobe Illustrator, Macintosh 9600/300 Power PC
paper/printing	Starwhite Vicksburg/Express Quality Printing & Lasercraft

design firm	**Hornall Anderson Design Works, Inc.**
art director	**Jack Anderson**
designers	**Jack Anderson, David Bates**
client	**Hornall Anderson Design Works, Inc.**
tool	**Macromedia FreeHand**
paper/printing	**French Durotone, Packing Grey Liner;**
	French Durotone, Newsprint White

design firm	**Vestígio, Lda.**
art director	**Emanuel Barbosa**
designer	**Emanuel Barbosa**
client	**Vestígo**
tools	**Macromedia FreeHand, Macintosh 8100 Power PC**
paper/printing	**Favini/Two color**

Vestígio: Consultores de Design, Lda.
Edifício Hoechst, Av. Sidónio Pais, 379, Salas 4-5
P-4100 Porto, Portugal
Tel. 02. 6064117 **Fax** 02. 6064117

design firm	**Roslyn Eskind Associates Limited**
art director	**Roslyn Eskind**
designer	**Roslyn Eskind**
client	**Roslyn Eskind Associates Limited**
tools	**Quark XPress, Adobe Photoshop, Adobe Illustrator, Macintosh**
paper/printing	**Chartham/Seaway Printing**

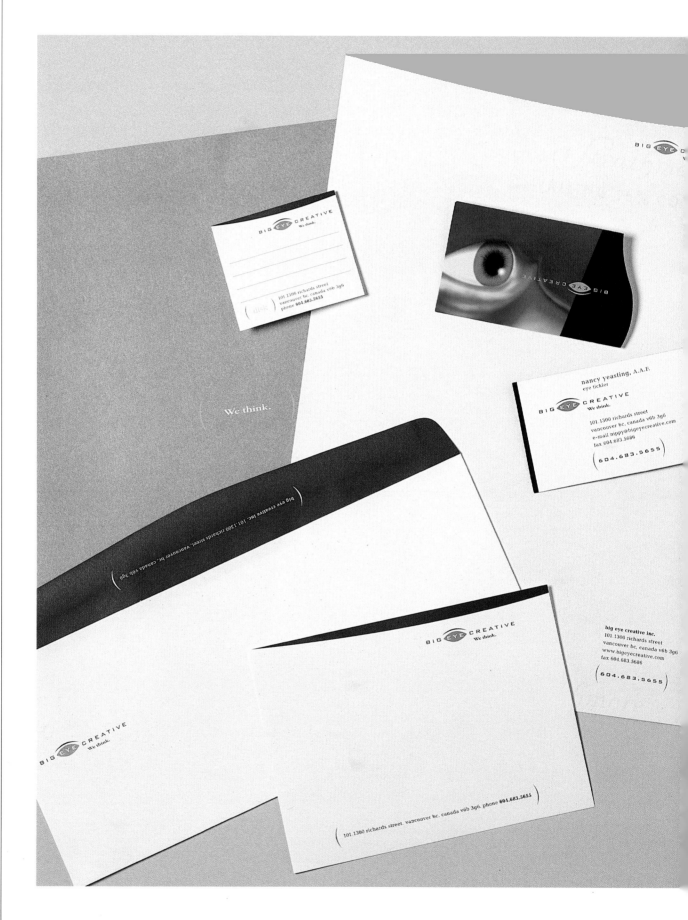

design firm	**Big Eye Creative, Inc.**
art director	**Perry Chua**
designer	**Perry Chua**
client	**Big Eye Creative, Inc.**
tools	**Adobe Illustrator 6.0, Adobe Photoshop 4.0, Macintosh**
paper/printing	**Cards: 120 lb. McCoy, Rest: Strathmore Writing/Clarke Printing**

RICHARDS ● DESIGN GROUP INC

5616 Kingston Pike, Suite 105
Knoxville, Tennessee 37919-6325

Post Office Box 10773
Knoxville, Tennessee 37939-0773

423-588-9707 Telephone
423-584-7741 Facsimile

www.richardsdesign.com

design firm	**Richards Design Group, Inc.**
art director	**Michael Richards**
designer	**Timothy D. Jenkins**
client	**Richards Design Group**
tools	**Adobe Illustrator, Quark XPress**
paper/printing	**Strathmore Soft White Wove/Ullrich Printing**

Timothy D. Jenkins / Designer

RICHARDS ● DESIGN GROUP INC

5616 Kingston Pike, Suite 105
Knoxville, Tennessee 37919-6325

Post Office Box 10773
Knoxville, Tennessee 37939-0773

423-588-9707 Telephone
423-584-7741 Facsimile

tjenkins@richardsdesign.com

design firm	Visual Dialogue
art director	Fritz Klaetke
designer	Fritz Klaetke
client	Edana Reps
tools	Quark XPress, Adobe Photoshop, Macintosh Power PC
paper/printing	Strathmore Writing & Labor Stock/Alpha Press

design firm	**Karacters Design Group**
creative director	**Maria Kennedy**
designer	**Matthew Clark**
client	**Karacters Design Group**
tools	**Adobe Illustrator, Quark XPress,**
	Adobe Photoshop, Macintosh
paper/printing	**Classic Crest/Hemlock Printing**

Twenty-five
Corporate Dr
Suite 218
Burlington
MA 01803

Phone 781·
273·2999

Fax 781·
273·3733

www.exhibit-a.com
eac@exhibit-a.com

design firm	**Exhibit A Communications**
art director	**Mark Gedrich**
designer	**Mark Gedrich**
client	**Exhibit A Communications**
tools	**Adobe Illustrator, Macintosh 9500 Power PC**

design firm	Burn World-Wide, Ltd.
art director	David L. Clarke
designer	Burn Staff
client	Burn World-Wide, Ltd.
tools	Adobe Illustrator, Adobe Photoshop
paper/printing	Classic Columns Stucco 80lb. text
	Haff and Duagherty, Miami, FL

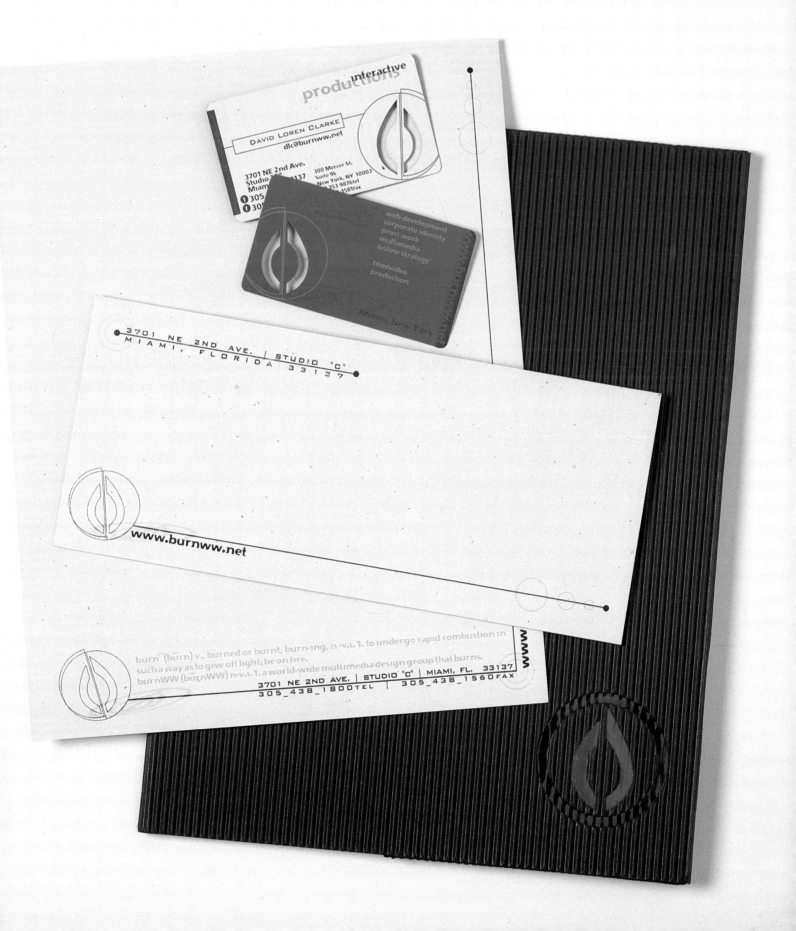

digital image magic

2 Magnolia Avenue
San Anselmo Ca 94960

phone   415 453 2828
fax   415 453 0828
e-mail   mail@lightrain.com

design firm | **be**
art director | **William Burke**
designers | **Eric Read, Coralie Russo**
client | **Light Rain**
tools | **Adobe Photoshop, Adobe Illustrator**

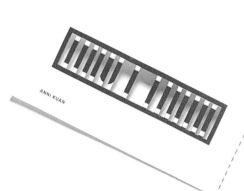

ANNI KUAN

242 W 38TH ST NEW YORK NY 10018 PHONE 212 704 4038 FAX 704 0651

design firm	Sagmeister Inc.
art director	Stefan Sagmeister
designers	Stefan Sagmeister/Hjalti Karlsson
client	Anni Kuan Design
tools	Adobe Illustrator/Macintosh 9500 Power PC
paper/printing	Strathmore Writing/ Offset, Laser Die-Cut

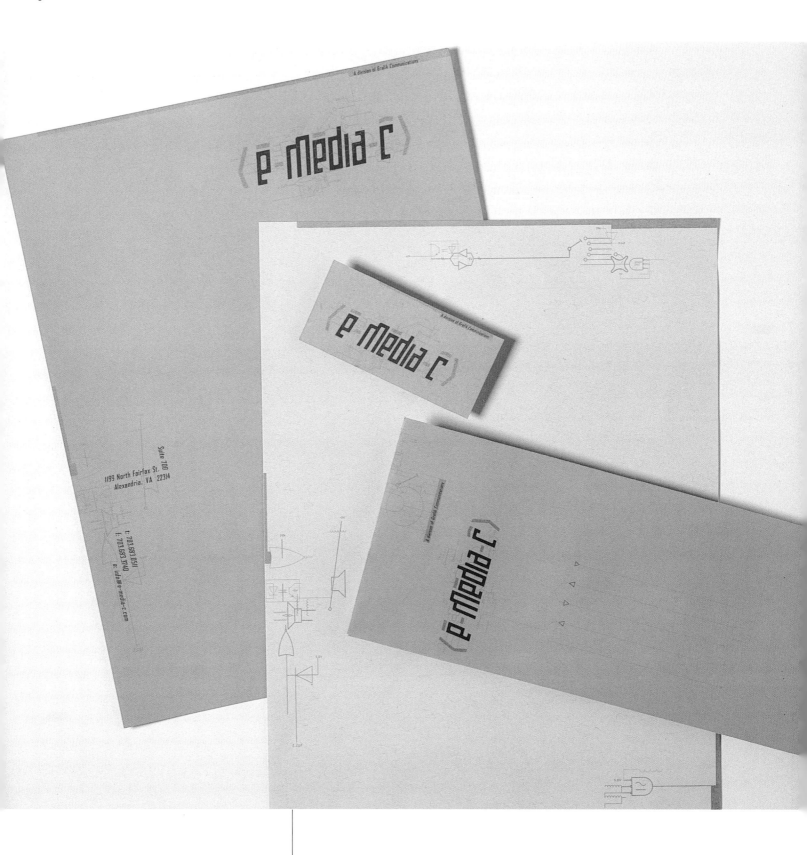

design firm	Grafik Communications, Ltd.
design team	Jonathan Amen, Eric Goetz
illustrator	Jonathan Amen
client	E-Media-C
tools	Macromedia FreeHand, Quark XPress
paper/printing	French Construction Fuse Green & Cement Green

MIRIELLO
GRAFICO
Graphic Communication

design firm	Miriello Grafico, Inc.
art director	Ron Miriello
designer	Ron Miriello
client	Miriello Grafico, Inc.
tools	Adobe Illustrator, Adobe Photoshop, Macintosh
paper/printing	Gilbert Esse/Offset litho four-color over two-color, hand-perforated edging, embossed

MIRIELLO
GRAFICO, INC.
Graphic Communication

419 WEST G STREET, SAN DIEGO, CALIFORNIA 92101, 619 234-1124 · FAX 619 234-1960
VIA DALMAZIA, 4-31044 MONTEBELLUNA (TREVISO) ITALY, 0423/600310 (R.A.) FAX 0423/303365

MIRIELLO
GRAFICO
Graphic Communication

RON MIRIELLO

419 WEST G STREET
SAN DIEGO, CALIFORNIA 92101
619 234-1124 · FAX 234-1960

PREMIER

design firm | Elixir Design, Inc.
art director | Jennifer Jerde
designer | Michael Braley
client | Premier
tool | Adobe Illustrator

JABRA

design firm | Mires Design
art director | Scott Mires
designer | Miguel Perez
illustrator | Miguel Perez
client | Jabra Corporation

JONELLE WEAVER

STUDIO
GG CROSBY #5D NEW YORK NEW YORK 10012
PHONE AND FAX 800-915-9331

OFFICE
268 HENRY STREET #2F BROOKLYN HEIGHTS NEW YORK 11201
PHONE AND FAX 800-915-9331

design firm	Elixir Design, Inc.
art director	Jennifer Jerde
designer	Jennifer Tolo
client	Jonelle Weaver
tools	Quark XPress, Adobe Illustrator
paper/printing	Scallop-edged placement stock

Latido

Mónica Braga

Reciclável e impresso em papel reciclado
Colabore na protecção da Natureza

Latido, Animais e afins, Lda.
Lugar das Teixugueiras
S. Miguel das Caldas
Tel. 053. 585884
P.4815 Caldas de Vizela
Portugal

U.S. CIGAR
SINCE 1883
SALES, INC.

ROBIN STRUYVE
Director of Cigar Mari
11 NE 145th Street, Woodinville, WA 98072
P: 425·488·1133   F: 425·488·4688

CAFE

retail, restaurant, and hospitaliy

5850

Ellsworth

Avenue

Pittsburgh

Pennsylvania

15232

design firm | **Brabender Cox**
art director | **Stephen Smith**
designer | **Stephen Smith**
client | **ICON/Sports rock entertainment**
tool | **Adobe Illustrator**

design firm | Hornall Anderson Design Works, Inc.
art director | Hornall Anderson Design Works, Inc.
designers | Larry Anderson, Mary Hermes,
| Mike Calkins, Michael Brugman
client | U.S. Cigar
tools | Macromedia FreeHand

design firm	Barbara Chan Design
art director	Barbara Chan
designer	Barbara Chan
client	Recess
tools	Adobe Illustrator 7.0, Macintosh G3

design firm	Kirima Design Office
art director	Harumi Kirima
designer	Harumi Kirima
client	Happy-En

design firm | Jim Lange Design
art director | Lee Langill
designer | Jim Lange
client | Lee Langill
tool | Macintosh

design firm | Murrie Lienhart Rysner
art director | Linda Voll
designer | Linda Voll
client | Wellness Business Works
tool | Adobe Illustrator

design firm	Teviot
art director	Kate Laing
designer	Jim Ramsay
client	Teviot
tools	Quark XPress, Adobe Illustrator 6.0
paper/printing	Arjo Wiggins Hi-Five-Cyber/One-color lithography

J. MELVILLE ENGLE
PRESIDENT,
CHIEF EXECUTIVE OFFICER

TEL: 781.932.6616
EXT. 106

ANIKA THERAPEUTICS, INC.
236 WEST CUMMINGS PARK
WOBURN, MA 01801

FAX: 781.932.3360
E-MAIL: MENGLE@
ANIKATHERAPEUTICS.COM

design firm	**Ellis Pratt Design, Inc.**
art director	**Vernon Ellis**
designer	**Elaine Pratt**
client	**Anika Therapeutics, Inc.**
tools	**Adobe Illustrator, Macintosh G3**
paper/printing	**Strathmore Writing/Maran Printing**

393 *Totten Pond Road*
Waltham, MA 02451
(781)487-9996 *direct*
(781)487-9997 *fax*
(877)363-9463 *gift orders*
SENDWINE.COM *website*

design firm	Phillips Design Group
art director	Steve Phillips
designers	Alison Goudreault, Susan Logher
client	Sendwine.com
tools	Adobe Illustrator 7.0, Macintosh G3
paper/printing	Strathmore Writing, Soft White/ BHF Printing

MIKE LANNON
President & Founder

393 *Totten Pond Road*
Waltham, MA 02451
(781)487-9996 *direct*
(781)487-9997 *fax*
(877)363-9463 *gift orders*
MIKE@SENDWINE.COM

design firm	**Arrowstreet Graphic Design**
art director	**Bob Lowe**
designer	**Seth Londergan**
client	**Pet Corner, LLC**
tools	**Adobe Illustrator, Macintosh Power PC**
paper/printing	**Poseidon White/Direct Printing**

A Z A L E A
R E S T A U R A N T

3612 BROWNSBORO ROAD
LOUISVILLE. KY 40207
TELEPHONE (502) 895-5493
FACSIMILE (502) 895-4822

design firm | Choplogic
art director | Walter McCord
designers | Walter McCord, Mary Cawein
client | Azalea
paper/printing | Simpson Antiqua/One-color lithography

A MILLION A WEEK
BACK TO THE COMMUNITY

COMMUNITY RELATIONS DEPT.

Target Stores   33 South Sixth Street   Minneapolis, MN 55402

COMMUNITY RELATIONS

Target Stores   33 South Sixth Street   Minneapolis, MN 55402

design firm	Design Guys
art director	Steven Sikora
designers	Anne Peterson, Tom Riddle
client	Target Stores
tool	Quark XPress
paper/printing	80 lb. Strathmore Writing/Challenge Printing

design firm	Vestígio
art director	Emanuel Barbosa
designer	Emanuel Barbosa
client	Latido
tool	Macromedia FreeHand
paper/printing	Renova Print/Two-color offset

Latido

Mónica Braga

Latido, Animais e afins, Lda.
Lugar das Teixugueiras
S. Miguel das Caldas
Tel. 053. 585884
P-4815 Caldas de Vizela
Portugal

Reciclável e impresso em papel reciclado   Colabore na protecção da Natureza

Latido, Animais e afins, Lda.
Lugar das Teixugueiras
S. Miguel das Caldas
P-4815 Caldas de Vizela
Tel. 053. 585884
Portugal

Reciclável e impresso em papel reciclado   Colabore na protecção da Natureza

Name	RALPH ALTHOFF		PHON	·49 (0) 821 - 59 29 58		
			PHAX	·49 (0) 821 - 59 29 58		
Adress	Alpenstraße 18	Bank	BfG Bank AG Augsburg			Logo
	86159 Augsburg		BLZ 720 10 J11			
	Germany		Kto 1422 6775 00	NO:	763	

RENT A BAR
Cocktails

» » **RENT A BARMAN** · Ralph Althoff · Alpenstraße 18 · 86159 Augsburg

» **RENT A BAR VERANSTALTUNGSSERVICE** «

design firm	**Marius Fahrner**
art director	**Marius Fahrner**
designer	**Marius Fahrner**
client	**'Rent a Bar' Barservice**
tools	**Adobe Illustrator, Quark XPress**
paper/printing	**Römerturm Countryside/**
	Schickinger Werbedrull 2/0

design firm	Vrontikis Design Office
art director	Petrula Vrontikis
designers	Christina Hsaio, Stationary: Petrula Vrontikis
client	Kozo Hasegawa, Global Dining, Inc.
tools	Adobe Photoshop, Quark XPress
paper/printing	Crosspointe Synergy/Login Printing

1212 3rd Street Promenade

Santa Monica, CA 90401

fax: (310) 576-9988
www.global-dining.com

phone: (310) 576-9996

design firm	Mires Design
art director	John Ball
designers	John Ball, Miguel Perez, and Jeff Samaripa
client	dab fragrance sampling

Letterhead and Logo 6 |

DIVAN

7661 GIRARD AVE. LA JOLLA, CALIFORNIA 92037 **PH 619.551.0405 FAX 619.551.0639**

design firm	**Miriello Grafico, Inc.**
art director	**Ron Miriello**
designer	**Courtney Mayer**
client	**Divan**
tools	**Adobe Illustrator, Adobe Photoshop, Macintosh**
printing	**Offset litho three color over two color**

boston light source

Architectural L
Manufacturer's

·64 commercial wharf, BOSTON, Massachusetts 02110-3808

FAX: 617.367.0925

WEB: www.bostonligr

boston light source

ROBERT A EDWARDS

Architectural Lighting
Manufacturer's Representative

64 commercial wharf, BOSTON, MA 02110-3808

WEB: www.bostonlightsource.com

PHONE: 617.367.0910 x234 FAX: 617 367.0925

EMAIL: redwards.bls@lighting.net

n light source

64 commercial wharf, BOSTON, MA 02110-3808

boston light source

64 commercial wharf, BOSTON, MA 02110-3808

Representing manufacturers offering products with a perceptible
advantage for the coordination of lighting with architecture.

design firm | Korn Design
art director | Denise Korn
designer | Christine Brooks
client | Boston Light Source
tools | Adobe Illustrator, Quark XPress
paper/printing | Alpha Press

HOOCH & HOLLY'S
SEASIDE BISTRO

P.O. BOX 1409
DOWNTOWN, ROUTE I
OGUNQUIT, ME / 03907

T: (207) 646-HOOCH
F: (207) 646-5617

design firm	Korn Design
art director	Denise Korn
designers	Jenny Pelzek, Javier Cortés
client	Hooch & Holly's Restaurant
tools	Adobe Illustrator, Quark XPress, Macintosh Power PC
paper/printing	Classic Crest - Neenah/Alpha Press

recreation and entertainment

401 Richmond St.W. Suite 104 Toronto.Ontario.Canada M5V 1X3 phone (416) 340-8869 fax 340-9819

design firm	**Cuppa Coffee Animation**
art director	**Adam Shaheen**
designer	**Julian Grey**
client	**Cuppa Coffee Animation**
paper/printing	**Central Printing**

design firm	Brabender Cox
art director	Stephen Smith
designer	Stephen Smith
client	Breed Records
tool	Adobe Illustrator

design firm	what!design
art director	Damon Meibers
designer	Damon Meibers
client	Clearcut Recording
tools	Adobe Illustrator, Quark XPress
paper/printing	Atlas Printing

design firm	Blok Design
art director	Vanessa Eckstein
designer	Vanessa Eckstein
client	Industry Films
tools	Adobe Illustrator, Quark XPress
paper/printing	Strathmore Ultimate White/Offset

design firm | Mires Design
art director | John Ball
designers | John Ball, Miguel Perez
illustrator | Tracy Sabin
client | Nike Inc.

design firm | Mires Design
art director | John Ball
designers | John Ball, Deborah Hom
client | Nike, Inc.

design firm	DogStar Design
art director	Jennifer Martin
designer	Jennifer Martin
client	Roaring Tiger Films
tool	Macromedia FreeHand

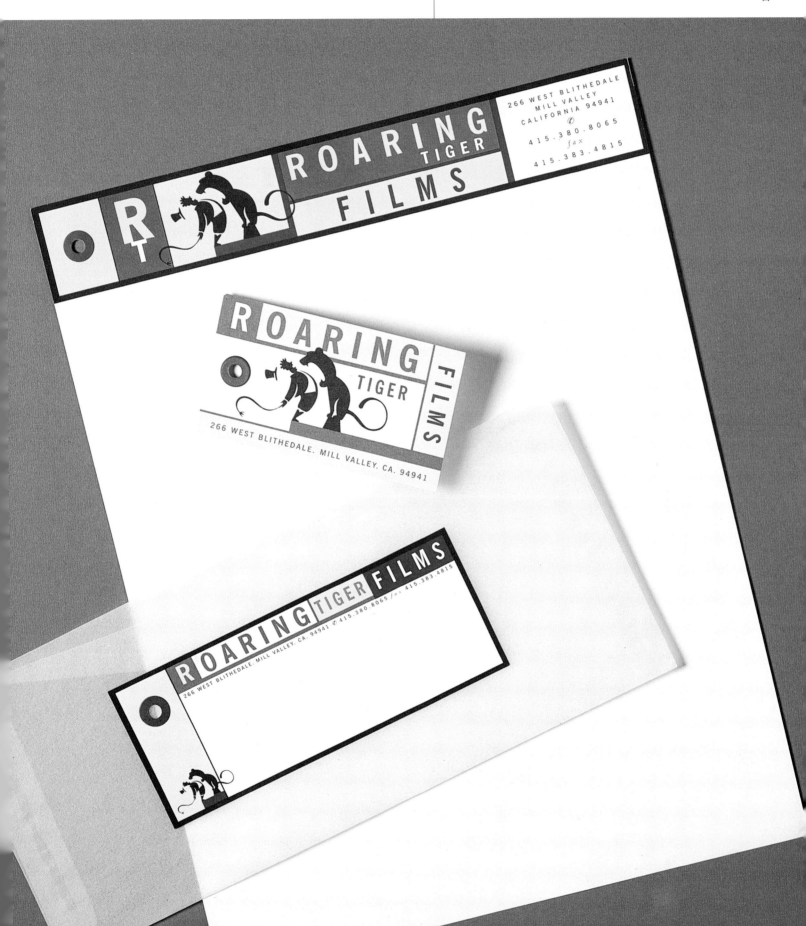

design firm	The Riordon Design Group, Inc.
art director	Ric Riordon
designers	Dan Wheaton, Sharon Porter
client	Free TV
tools	Adobe Illustrator, Quark XPress, Adobe Photoshop
paper/printing	Bravo/Contact Creative

design firm	Iron Design
art director	Todd Edmonds
designer	Jim Keller
client	Ripcord Games
tool	Adobe Illustrator
paper/printing	Strathmore/Four-color process, metallic silver

www.peterpan.com

973.344.4214 Tel

973.344.0465 Fax

PPI Entertainment 88 Saint Francis St. Newark NJ 07105

Henry Moyer
National Sales Manager,
Audio

88 Saint Francis St.
Newark, NJ 07105

973.344.4214
973.344.2233 Fax

www.peterpan.com

PPI Entertainment

PPI Entertainment

design firm	Iron Design
art director	Todd Edmonds
designer	Ted Skibinski
client	PPI Entertainment
tools	Adobe Dimensions, Adobe Illustrator
paper/printing	Mohawk/Four-color process, metallic silver

design firm | Mires Design
art director | Jose Serrano
designers | Jose Serrano, Miguel Perez
client | Hell Racer

design firm | Mires Design
art director | Jose Serrano
designers | Jose Serrano, Miguel Perez
client | Hell Racer

design firm | **Jim Lange Design**
art director | **Kathleen Hughes**
designer | **Jim Lange**
client | **Public Library Association conference logo**
tool | **Macintosh**

design firm | **Karacters Design Group**
designer | **Maria Kennedy**
client | **Eaglequest Golf Centers**

Neil Lupkes
Maintenance

Pacific Golf
8080 Center Street S.W.
Tumwater
Washington
98501
Telephone:
(360) 786-8626
Facsimile:
(360) 786-8626
www.eaglequestgolf.com

Learn. Practice. Play.

Learn. Practice. Play.

e. Play.

eag**f**equest
GOLF CENTERS

eag**f**equest   Learn. Practice. Play.

Del Roy Drive

las

Texas

75229

Direct Line:

(214) 706-6925

Facsimile:

(214) 706-6924

www.eaglequestgolf.com

design firm | **Art Chantry Design Company**
designer | **Art Chantry**
client | **Estrus Records**

design firm | Art Chantry Design Company
designer | Art Chantry
client | The Showbox

design firm | Art Chantry Design Company
designer | Art Chantry
client | Estrus Records

PAY-OUTS

design firm | Art Chantry Design Company
designer | Art Chantry
client | Estrus Records

design firm | Art Chantry Design Company
designer | Art Chantry
client | Hell's Elevator Productions

HELL'S ELEVATOR PROD.

design firm | **Art Chantry Design Company**
designer | **Art Chantry**
client | **Empty Records**

design firm | Sametz Blackstone Associates
art director | Will Cook
designer | Will Cook
client | Provincetown Repertory Theatre
tools | Macintosh Power PC, Quark XPress,
Adobe Photoshop, Infinity

design firm	Vrontikis Design Office
art director	Petrula Vrontikis
designers	Victor Corpuz, Stationary: Winnie Li
client	Mama Records
tools	Quark XPress, Adobe Illustrator
paper/printing	Champion Benefit/Login Printing

THE LIONEL CORPORATION   50625 RICHARD W. BOULEVARD   TELEPHONE 810.949.4100   FACSIMILE 810.949.3273
CHESTERFIELD, MICHIGAN
48051-2493

design firm	**Michael Stanard Design**
art directors	**Michael Stanard, Marc Fuhrman**
designers	**Michael Chang, Marc Fuhrman**
client	**Lionel, LLC**
tools	**Adobe Illustrator, Macintosh**
paper/printing	**Strathmore Writing/**
	Offset lithography

design firm	Jim Lange Design
art director	Jan Caille
designer	Jim Lange
client	Mrs. T's Chicago Triathlon
tools	Macintosh, Hand illustration
paper/printing	Smith Printing

design firm	Sametz Blackstone Associates
art director	Robert Beerman
designer	Hania Khuri
client	90.9 WBUR/The Connection
tools	Quark XPress, Adobe Photoshop, Macintosh Power PC
paper/printing	24 lb. Strathmore Writing Bright White/Puritan Press

90.9 WBUR
890 Commonwealth Avenue
Boston, Massachusetts
02215

617 353.2790
617 353.8147 fax

90.9 WBUR
Boston University
890 Commonwealth Avenue
Boston, Massachusetts
02215

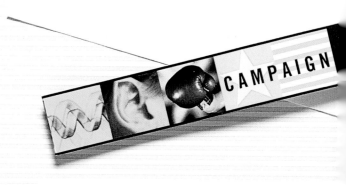

JJ Suthe
Produce

the co

90.9 WBUR   617 35
890 Commonwealth Ave.   617 35
Boston, Massachusetts   617 35
02215   jj.suthe

The Conn

design firm	Segura, Inc.
art director	Carols Segura
designer	Colin Metcalf
client	Q101 Radio
tools	Adobe Photoshop, Adobe Illustrator
paper/printing	MTG Productions

Festival Bay

design firm	Selbert Perkins Design
art director	Robin Perkins
design director	Greg Welch
designers	John Lutz, Ingrid Langhout, Julie D'Andrea
client	The Jerde Partnership International, Inc.

design firm	Selbert Perkins Design
art directors	Robin Perkins, Clifford Selbert
designers	Gemma Lawson, Heather Watson
client	The Jerde Partnership International, Inc.

70 UNIVERSAL CITY PLAZA   UNIVERSAL CITY, CALIFORNIA   USA   91608   818.777.4000 т   WWW.MCARECORDS.COM

design firm	Segura, Inc.
art director	Carlos Segura
designers	Carlos Segura,
	Susana Detembleque
client	MCA
tools	Adobe Photoshop, Adobe Illustrator

design firm | **Simon & Goetz Design**
art director | **Ruediger Goetz**
designer | **Ruediger Goetz**
illustrator | **Manuela Schmidt**
client | **ZDF**

design firm | Simon & Goetz Design
art director | Ruediger Goetz
designer | Ruediger Goetz
illustrator | Elke Boehm
client | ZDF

design firm | Simon & Goetz Design
art director | Ruediger Goetz
designers | Beth Martin, Jorge Waldschuetz
client | Helkon Media Filmvertries GMBH

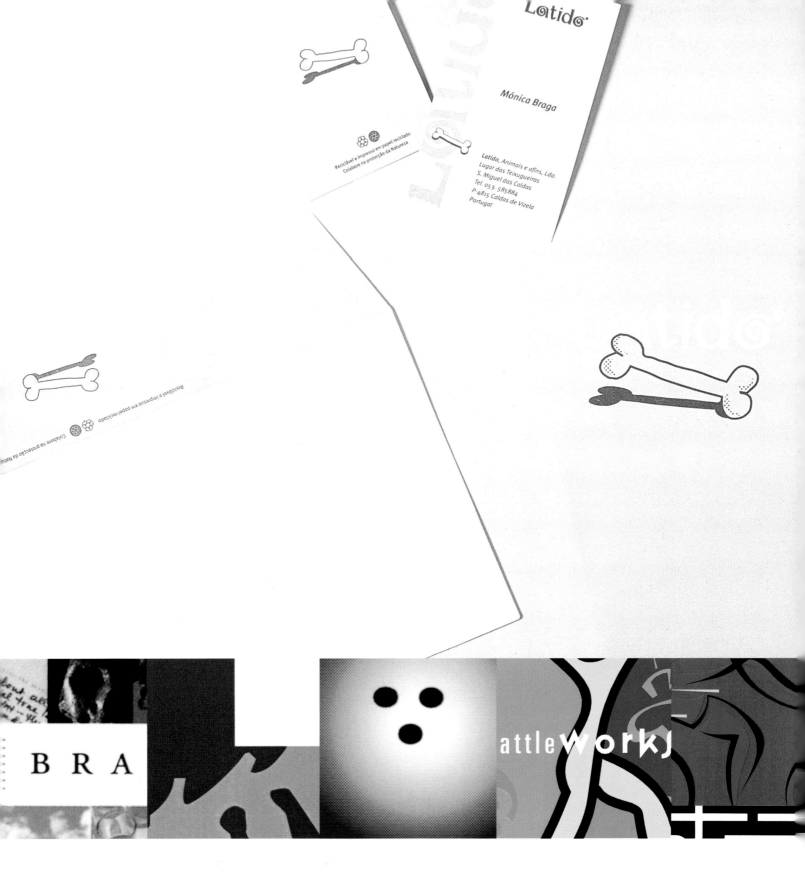

education, health, and non-profit

SEATTLE TO PORTLAND BICYCLE CLASSIC

design firm	That's Cadiz! Originals
art director	Mineleo Cadiz
designer	Mineleo Cadiz
client	Cascade Bicycle Club
tool	Macromedia FreeHand 8.0

design firm	That's Cadiz! Originals
art director	Mineleo Cadiz
designer	Mineleo Cadiz
client	Seattle Marathon Association
tool	Macromedia FreeHand 8.0

Design Milwaukee
Milwaukee Institute of Art & Design

273 East Erie Street Milwaukee, Wisconsin 53202 Phone 414 276 7889 Facsimile 414 291 8078

Building awareness of
design in Wisconsin

design firm	**Becker Design**
art director	**Neil Becker**
designer	**Neil Becker**
client	**Design Milwaukee**
tool	**Quark XPress**

Design Milwaukee
Milwaukee Institute of Art & Design

Building awareness of design in Wisconsin

design firm	Walker Pinfold Associates London
art director	Catherine Thomas
designer	Clare Wilson
client	Lampeter University-Australian Studies
tools	Quark XPress, Adobe Illustrator
paper/printing	Zanders Lana Graphic/Two-color lithography

design firm	Sayles Graphic Design
art director	John Sayles
designer	John Sayles
client	Goodtime Jazz Festival
tool	Macintosh
paper/printing	Neenah Bond/Offset

BOCATRIOL®
calcitriol

design firm | Leo Pharmaceutical Products
art director | Martin Isbrand
designer | Martin Isbrand
client | Leo Pharmaceutical Products

K L S O

design firm | Werk-Haus
designers | Ezrah Rahim, Paggie Chin Lee Choo
client | Kuala Lumpur Symphony Orchestra Society
tool | Macintosh

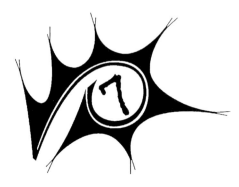

Seven Tepees Youth Program

design firm | Patricia Bruning Design
art director | Patricia Bruning
designers | Patricia Bruning, Fran Terry
client | Seven Tepees Youth Program
tools | Quark XPress 3.32, Adobe Illustrator 6.0, Macintosh 7100 Power PC
paper/printing | Hamilton Press

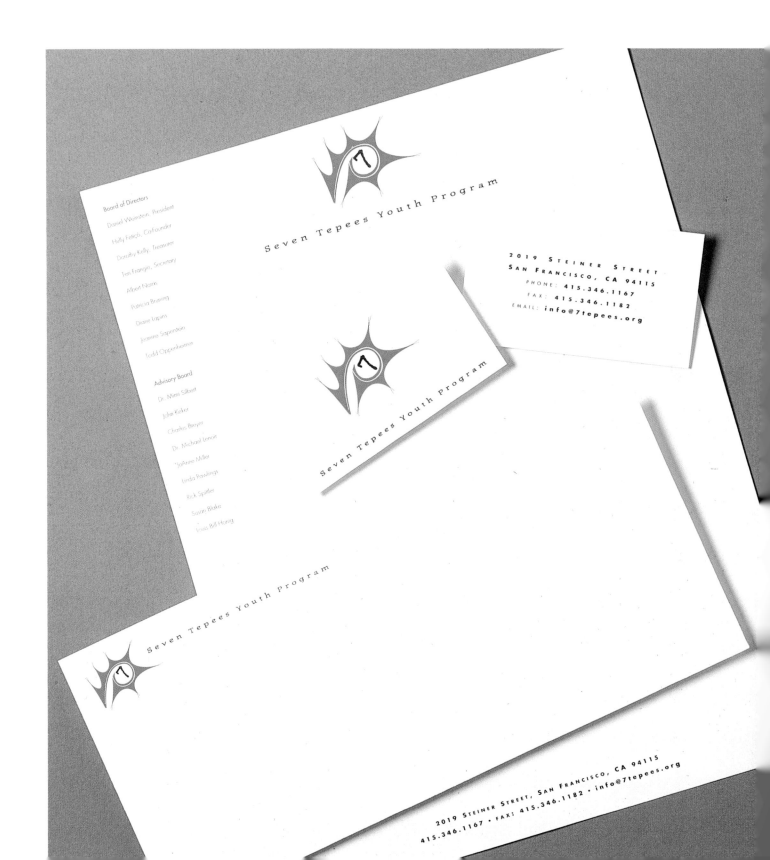

HARVARD UNIVERSITY

220 Longwood Avenue
Goldenson 526
Boston, Massachusetts 02115

HARVARD UNIVERSITY

220 Longwood Avenue
Goldenson 526
Boston, Massachusetts 02115

design firm	**Visual Dialogue**
art director	**Fritz Klaetke**
designers	**Fritz Klaetke, David Kraljic**
client	**Harvard University**
tools	**Quark XPress, Adobe Photoshop, Macintosh Power PC**
paper/printing	**Strathmore Elements/Color Express**

design firm | The Point Group
designer | David Howard
client | Big Brothers & Big Sisters of Dallas
tool | Adobe Illustrator

SUMMIT 1999

design firm | Leo Pharmaceutical Products
art director | Martin Isbrand
designer | Martin Isbrand
client | Leo Pharmaceutical Products

design firm	Vanderbyl Design
art director	Michael Vanderbyl
designers	Michael Vanderbyl, Erica Wilcott
client	The American Center for Wine, Food & the Arts
tools	Quark XPress, Adobe Illustrator
paper/printing	Cranes Crest/Trade Engraving

PEGGY A. LOAR
DIRECTOR

FRANCES A. ANAMOSA
EXECUTIVE ASSISTANT
1700 SOSCOL AVE SUITE 1 NAPA CA 94559
TEL 707·257·3606 FAX 707·257·8601
EMAIL: fanamosa@theamericancenter.org

THE AMERICAN CENTER
FOR WINE, FOOD & THE ARTS
1700 SOSCOL AVENUE SUITE 1
NAPA CALIFORNIA 9455
TEL 707·257·3606 FAX 707·

·606 FAX 707·257·8601

design firm	Sayles Graphic Design
art director	John Sayles
designer	John Sayles
client	Sue Roberts Health Concepts
tool	Macintosh
paper/printing	Neenah Environment Natural/Four-color offset

design firm	That's Cadiz! Originals
art director	Mineleo Cadiz
designer	Mineleo Cadiz
client	Seattle Works
tool	Macromedia FreeHand 8.0

design firm	Odeon Zwo
art director	Boris Eisenberg
designer	Dmitri Lavrow
client	Municipality of Hannover

Landeshauptstadt **Hannover**

Referat für
Gleichstellungsfragen
Frauenbüro

Dienstgebäude	Röselerstraße 2	30159 Hannover

Referat für
Gleichstellungsfragen - Frauenbüro | Postfach 125 | 30001 Hannover

Bearbeitet von	
TELEFON	0511 168	
FAX	0511 168	6699
Vermittlung	0511 168	0

Sprechzeiten	dienstags	15.00 - 17.00
	donnerstags	09.00 - 12.00
	und nach Vereinbarung	

Ihr Zeichen, Ihre Nachricht vom	Mein Zeichen (Bitte bei Antwort angeben)	Hannover
	10.13/	

Bankverbindungen der Stadtkasse	**BLZ**	**KONTO**
Stadtsparkasse Hannover	250 501 80	517 321
Deutsche Postbank AG Hannover	250 100 30	15 - 305
NordLB	250 500 00	101 359 818
Landeszentralbank in Niedersachsen	250 000 00	250 017 68

médiathèque la durance

rue Véran Rousset, BP 81
84303 Cavaillon Cedex
tél. 04 90 76 21 48, fax 04 90 78 06 71

design firm	**Made in mouse**
art director	**David Hairion**
designer	**Sandrine Langlet**
client	**Médiathèque de Cavaillon**
tools	**Macintosh Illustrator, Quark XPress**
paper/printing	**Rive/Offset**

miscellaneous

A M E R
I C A N
M A N I
C U R E

A M E R I C A N   M A N I C U R E   C O R P O R A T I O N
A   D I V I S I O N   O F   A M   L A B O R A T O R I E S ,   I N C .
2328 CENTERLINE INDUSTRIAL DRIVE   ST. LOUIS, MO 63146   314.432.0363 FAX 432.8535 1.800.782.3555

design firm	**Bartels & Company**
art director	**David Bartels**
designers	**Ron Rodemacher, Don Strandel**
client	**American Manicure**
tools	**Adobe Illustrator, Macintosh**
paper/printing	**Midwest Printing**

L A U R A   K R E T S C H M A R

A M E R
I C A N
M A N I
C U R E

2328 CENTERLINE INDUSTRIAL DR
ST. LOUIS, MO 63146   314.432.0363
FAX 314.432.8535 1.800.782.3555

design firm | Insight Design Communications
art directors | Tracy Holdeman, Sherrie Holdeman
designers | Tracy Holdeman, Sherrie Holdeman
client | Clotia Wood & Metal Works
tools | Macromedia FreeHand 7.0, Macintosh

design firm	Segura, Inc.
art director	Carlos Segura
designer	Carlos Segura
client	[T-26]
tool	Adobe Illustrator
paper/printing	Mohawk/Rohner Letterpress

design firm | **After Hours Creative**
designer | **After Hours Creative**
client | **Just One**

design firm | Synergy Design
designer | Leon Alvarado
client | Mega Estacíon
tools | Macromedia FreeHand,
Macintosh
paper/printing | Various

THE FINE LINE

design firm | Murrie Lienhart Rysner
art director | Linda Voll
designer | Linda Voll
client | The Fine Line
tools | Adobe Illustrator

Schwer Präzision GmbH   Hauptstraße 148   D - 78588 Denkingen

Schwer Präzision GmbH	Telefon	Registergericht Tuttlingen	Kreissparkasse Spaichingen
Drehteile u. Techn. Produkte	07424 / 98 15-0	HRB 571 Sp. Sitz: Denkingen	643 500 70 Kto 455 095
Hauptstraße 148	Fax	Geschäftsführer: Klaus Schwer	Raiffeisenbank Denkingen
D - 78588 Denkingen	07424 / 98 15-30	USt.-Id.-Nr. DE 811731829	643 626 13 Kto 50 444 000

design firm | revoLUZion
art director | Bernd Luz
designer | Bernd Luz
client | Schwer Präzision
tools | Macromedia FreeHand, Macintosh

design firm | **Russell, Inc.**
art director | **Bob Russell**
client | **Cancom, Inc.**

HealthSat

50 Burnhamthorpe
Road West
10th floor
Mississauga
Ontario
L5B 3C2

TELEPHONE
(905) 803-0500
1-800-263-9509
FACSIMILE
(905) 272-6680

Alain Gourd
President and
Chief Executive
Officer

design firm	Segura, Inc.
art director	Carlos Segura
designer	Carlos Segura
client	Blue Rock
tools	Adobe Photoshop, Adobe Illustrator

DETERMAN BROWNIE, INC.

· 1241 72ND AVENUE NORTHEAST ·
MINNEAPOLIS, MN 55432

PHONE: 612.571.8110

B

FAX: 612.571.1789

design firm	Design Center
art director	John Reger
designer	Jon Erickson
client	Determan Brownie, Inc.
tools	Macromedia FreeHand, Macintosh
paper/printing	Strathmore Writing/ Wallace Carlson

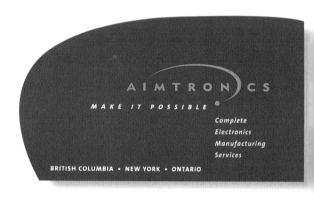

design firm	Big Eye Creative
art directors	Perry Chua, Nancy Yeasting
designers	Perry Chua, Nancy Yeasting
client	Aimtronics Corporation
tools	Adobe Illustrator, Macintosh Power PC
paper/printing	Cards: McCoy Silk, Rest: Classic Printing

AIMTRONICS CORPORATION

100 Schneider Road
Kanata, Ontario
Canada K2K 1Y2
tel 613.592.2240
fax 613.592.9449

ONTARIO

NEW YORK

BRITISH COLUMBIA

MAKE IT POSSIBLE

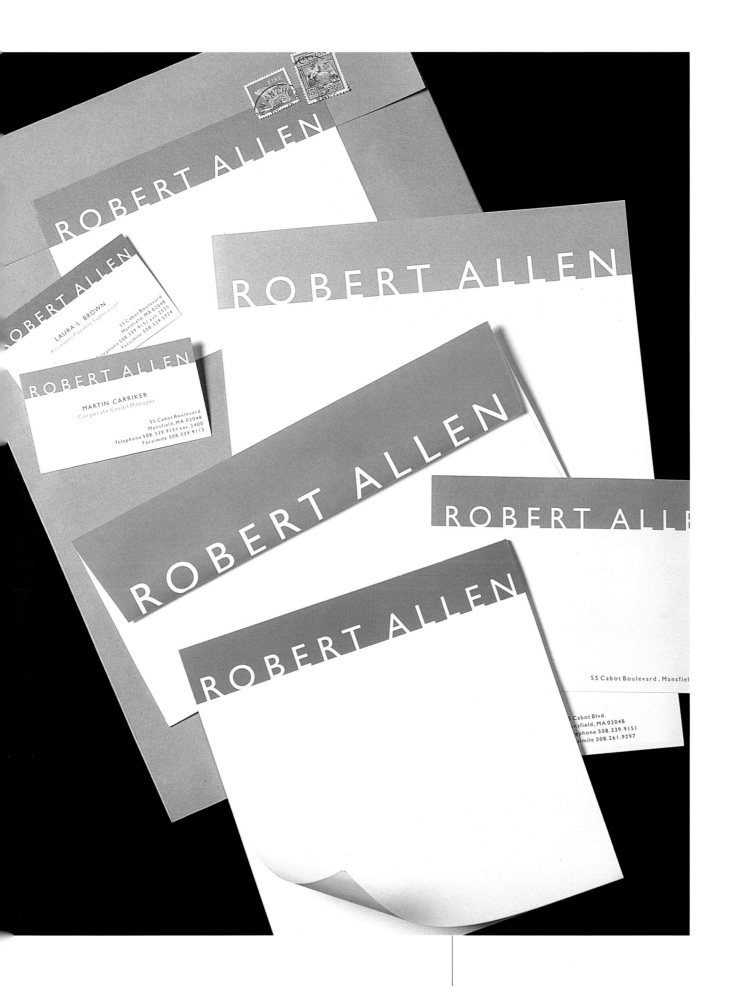

design firm	Slover and Company
art director	Susan Slover
designer	Tamara Behar
client	Robert Allen Contract Fabrics
tools	Adobe Illustrator, Quark XPress, Macintosh Power PC
paper/printing	Two-color offset

design firm | **Patricia Bruning Design**
art director | **Patricia Bruning**
designers | **Patricia Bruning, Fran Terry**
client | **Johnson Hoke**
tools | **Quark XPress 3.32, Adobe Illustrator 6.0, Macintosh 7100 Power PC**
paper/printing | **Golden Dragon Printing**

design firm	Stewart Monderer Design, Inc.
art director	Stewart Monderer
designer	Aime Lecusay
client	NBase-Xyplex
tools	Adobe Illustrator, Macintosh G3

design firm | Robert Bailey Incorporated
art director | Dan Franklin
designers | Dan Franklin, Connie Lightner
client | Junovia Distributing
tools | Macromedia FreeHand 7.0, Quark XPress
paper/printing | Classic Crest/ Michael's Printing

JUNOVIΛ

JUNOVIA DISTRIBUTING. LLC
DISTRIBUTOR *of* PREMIUM CIGARS & ACCESSORIES

8048 SW EDGEWATER DRIVE WEST ▮ WILSONVILLE. OREGON 97070 ▮ 503 694.6620 *tel/* ▮ 503 694.5094 *fax*

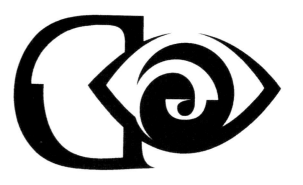

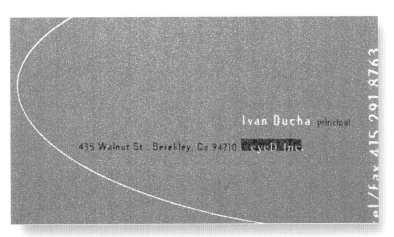

design firm	Cynthia Patten
art director	Cynthia Patten
designer	Cynthia Patten
client	Eye D
tools	Quark XPress 3.32, Adobe Illustrator 6.0, Macintosh 7100 Power PC
paper/printing	French Paper Frostone (Iceberg)/ Epson Ink Jet

Industrie-Vertretung
Rohloff

An der Schluse 23
D-48329 Havixbeck

Tel. 0 25 07 - 44 99
Fax 0 25 07 - 13 05

IVR Rohloff An der Schluse 23 D-48329 Havixbeck

Vertrieb elektronischer
Geräte und Systeme

design firm | **revoLUZion**
art director | **Bernd Luz**
designer | **Bernd Luz**
client | **IVR Rohloff**
tools | **Macromedia Freehand, Macintosh**

design firm	revoLUZion
art director	Bernd Luz
designer	Bernd Luz
client	revoLUZion/self
tools	Adobe Photoshop, Quark XPress, Macintosh

design firm	Elixir Design, Inc.
art director	Jennifer Jerde
designer	Nathan Durant
client	Perspecta
tool	Adobe Illustrator

design firm	Elixir Design, Inc.
art director	Jennifer Jerde
designer	Nathan Durant
client	Athleta
tool	Adobe Illustrator

design firm	Towers Perrin - Creative Media Group
art director	Jim Kohler
designer	Geoff Stone
client	Towers Perrin
tools	Quark Xpress, Adobe Photoshop, Adobe Illustrator, Macintosh

directory

AC/DC—Art Chantry
Design Company
P.O. Box 4069
Seattle, WA 98104

Acro Media, Inc.
431 Highway 33
Kelowna, BC
Canada

After Hours Creative
1201 East Jefferson B100
Phoenix, AZ 85034

Anne Gordon Design Pty. Ltd.
1 Caledonia Street
Paddington NSW 2021
Australia

Arrowstreet Graphic Design
212 Elm Street
Somerville, MA 02144

Art-Direction & Design
Schröderstiftstrasse 28
20146 Hamburg
Germany

Barabara Chan Design
614 South Saint Andrews, Suite 409
Los Angeles, CA 90005

Bartels and Company
3284 Ivanhoe Avenue
St. Louis, MO 63139

Becker Design
225 East St. Paul Avenue, Suite 300
Milwaukee, WI 53202

Belyea
1809 7th Avenue
Seattle, WA 98101

Big Eye Creative
101-1300 Richards Street
Vancouver, BC V68 3G6
Canada

Blok Design
398 Adelaide West, Suite 602
Toronto, Ontario M5V 2K4
Canada

Blue i Design
Imperial House
Lypiatt Road
Cheltenham GL50 2QJ
UK

Bob's Haus
3728 McKinley Boulevard
Sacramento, CA 95816

Brabender Cox
2100 Wharton Street
Pittsburgh, PA 15203

Choplogic
2014 Cherokee Parkway
Louisville, KY 40204

Cuppa Coffee Animation, Inc.
401 Richmond Street West, #104
Toronto, Ontario M5V IX3
Canada

Customized Communications Group
975 Middle Street, Suite B
Middletown, CT 06457

Design Center
15119 Minnetonka Boulevard
Mound, MN 55364

Design Guys
119 North Fourth Street, #400
Minneapolis, MN 55401

Designstudio CAW
Krugstrasse 16
30453 Hannover
Germany

DogStar Design
626 54th Street South
Birmingham, AL 35203

Earthlink Creative Services
3100 New York Drive
Pasadena, CA 91107

Ellis Pratt Design, Inc.
361 Newbury Street
Boston, MA 02115

Focus Design
and Marketing Solutions
3800 Valley Lights Drive
Pasadena, CA 91107

Giorgio Rocco Communications
Via Domenichino 27
20149 Milano
Italy

Gouthier Design
P.O. Box 840925
Hollywood, FL 33084

Grafik Communications, Ltd.
1199 North Fairfax Street, Suite 700
Alexandria, VA 22314

Greteman Group
142 North Mosley, 3rd Floor
Witchita, KS 67209

Hamagami/Carroll & Associates
1316 3rd Street
Promenade, #305
Santa Monica, CA 90401

Han/Davis Group
2933 North Sheridan, Apt. 1417
Chicago, IL 60657

Henderson Tyner Art Co.
315 N. Spruce Street, Suite 299
Winston-Salem, NC 27101

Hornall Anderson Design Works, Inc.
1008 Western Avenue, Suite 600
Seattle, WA 98104

Iconix Group
4927 Auburn Avenue
Bethesda, MD 20814

Insight Design Communication
322 South Mosley
Wichita, KS 67202

Iron Design
120 North Aurora Street, Suite 5A
Ithaca, NY 14850

Jim Lange Design
203 North Wabash Avenue
Chicago, IL 60601

João Machado Design, Lda
Rua Padre Xavier Coutinho,
125, 4150-371 Porto
Portugal

Karacters Design Group
1600-777 Hornby
Vancouver, BC
Canada

Kirima Design Office
5F, 1-5, Park-Bild, Yorikimachi
Yorikimachi, Kita-ku, Osaka-City
530-0036
Japan

Korn Design
22 Follen Street
Boston, MA 02116

Laughlin/Winkler, Inc.
4 Clarendon Street
Boston, MA 02116

Leo Pharmaceutical Products
Industriparken 55
Ballerup 2750
Denmark

Lima Design
215 Hanover Street
Boston, MA 02113

Lux Design
550 15th Street, #25A
San Francisco, CA 94103

Made in mouse
Moulin Priaulet BP 32
13520 Maussane
France

Marius Fahrner
Lastropsweg 5
20255 Hamburg
Germany

McGaughy Design
3706-A Steppes Court
Falls Church, VA 22041

Michael Stanard Design
1000 Main Street
Evanston, IL 60202

Mires Design
2345 Kettner Boulevard
San Diego, CA 92101

Modelhart Grafik-Design DA
A-5600 St. Johann/Pg Ing.
Ludwig Pech Str. 7
Austria

Moonlight Press Studio
362 Cromwell Avenue
Staten Island, NY 10305

Murrie Lienhart Rysner
325 West Huron Street
Chicago, IL 60607

Nesnady & Schwartz
10803 Magnolia Drive
Cleveland, OH 44106

Never Boring Design
1016 14th Street
Modesto, CA 95354

Nielinger Kommunikations design
Borsig str.5
45145 Essen
Germany

Oakley Design Studio
519 South West Park Avenue, Suite 521
Portland, OR 97205

Odeon Zwo
Odeonstr.2
D-30 59 Hannover
Germany

Parachute Design
120 S. 6th Street
Minneapolis, MN 55402

Patricia Bruning Design
1045 Sansome Street, Suite 219
San Francisco, CA 94111

Patten Design
55 Queensberry Street
Boston, MA 02215

Pham Phu Design
Hohenzollernstr.97
Munich 80796
Germany

Philips Design Group
25 Drydock Avenue
Boston, MA 02210

Planet Design Company
605 Williamson Street
Madison, WI 53703

Plum Notion Design Laboratory
140 Huyshope Avenue
Hartford, CT 06106

Prime Studio
326 7th Avenue
New York, NY 10001

Q Design
Neuberg 14
65193 Wiesbaden
Germany

revoLUZion
Uhlandstr. 4
78579 Neuhausen
Germany

Richards Design Group
5616 Kingston Park
Knoxville, TN 37919

Riordan Design Group
131 George Street
Oakville, Ontario
Canada

Robert Bailey, Inc.
0121 South West Bancroft Street
Portland, OR 97201

Roslyn Eskind Associates
471 Richmond Street West
Toronto, Ontario
Canada

Russell, Inc.
119 Spadina Avenue, Level 5,
Toronto, Ontario, M5V 2L1
Canada

Sametz Blackstone Associates
40 W. Newton Street
Boston, MA 02118

Sayegh Design
24734 Independence Drive, #3111
Farmington, MI 48333

Sayles Graphic Design
308 8th Street
Des Moines, IA 50309

Scott Stern
8 Minerva Way
Glasgow G38AU
UK

Segura, Inc.
1110 N. Milwaukee Avenue
Chicago, IL 60622

Seltzer Design
30 The Fenway
Boston, MA 02215

Shook Design Group
2000 South Boulevard, Suite 510
Charlotte, NC 28204

Slover and Company
584 Broadway, Suite 903
New York, NY 10001

Spin Productions, Inc.
620 King Street West
Totonto, Ontario
Canada

Square One Design
970 Monroe Avenue Northwest
Grand Rapids, MI 49503

Steven Curtis Design, Inc.
1807 West Sunnyside
Chicago, IL 60640

Stewart Monderer Design, Inc.
10 Thacher Street, Suite 112
Boston, MA 02113

Stoltze Design
49 Melcher Street, 4th Floor
Boston, MA 02210

Studio Bubblan
7:E Villagatan 28
50454 Boras
Sweden

Studio Hill: Design Ltd.
417 Second Street SW,
Ald. NM 87102
Synergy Design
600 Nottingham Oaks, #279
Houston, TX 77079

Synergy Design
600 Nottingham Oaks, Suite 279
Houston, TX 77079

Teviot
7 Dublin Street Lane South
Edinburgh EH1 3PX
UK

That's Cadiz! Originals
3823 14th Avenue West
Seattle, WA 98101

The Point Group
5949 Sherry Lane, Suite 1800
Dallas, TX 75225

Vanderbyl Design
171 2nd Street
San Francisco, CA 94109

Vestígio
Av. Sidónio Pais, 379,
Salas 4-5 P-4100 Porto
Portugal

Visual Dialogue
429 Columbus Avenue #1,
Boston, MA 02116

Vrontikis Design Office
2021 Pontius Pilot Avenue
Los Angeles, CA 90025

Walker Pinfold Associates London
17, The Ivories 6 Northampton Street
London NI 2HY
UK

Walker Thomas Associates
Top Floor, Osment Buildings
Maples Lane Prahran 3181
Australia

Warren Group
622 Hampton Drive
Venice, CA 90231

Werk-Haus
71-3 Medan Setia 1 Bukit Damansara
50490 Kuala Lumpur
Malaysia

what!design
119 Braintree
Allston, MA 02134

Woodworth Associates
151 Newbury Street
Portland, ME 04101

X Design Company
2525 West Main Street, #201
Littleton, CO 80120

index